Written by: Michael Haught, Wayne Turner, Phil Yates

Contributors: Alexander Costantino, Scott Elaurant, Sean Ireland, Dr. Michael McSwiney, Mitch Reed, Nathan Ward

Editors: Peter Simunovich, John-Paul Brisigotti

Proof Readers: Alexander Costantino, Mitch Kemmis, Michael McSwiney, Gary Martin, Gregg Siter, Stephen Smith

Graphic Design: Sean Goodison

Miniatures Design: Evan Allen, Tim Adcock

Cover Art: Vincent Wai

Miniatures Painting: Evan Allen, James Brown, Blake Coster, Michael Haught, Steve London, Aaron Mathie, Chris Townley

Terrain Modelling and Photography: Battlefront Studio

Playtest Groups: Dad's Army (Gavin van Rossum), Houston (Mike Callahan), Northern Battle Gamers (Nigel Slater).

CONTENTS

This is a supplement for *Flames Of War, the World War II miniatures game.*
A copy of the rulebook for *Flames Of War* is necessary to fully use the contents of this book.

THE GREAT WAR

The Great War of 1914-18 was global in its reach. The large empires of the main European powers meant that conflicts occurred in places as diverse as East Asia, Africa, and off the coast of South America. Yet this global conflict would be decided by the mighty clashes upon the battlefields of Europe.

House of Cards

After Austrian Archduke Franz Ferdinand was assassinated in Sarajevo, Bosnia on 28 June 1914, an elaborate system of secret treaties and agreements unfolded. Russia backed Serbia, Germany backed Austria-Hungary, France honoured its agreement with Russia and declared war against Germany, which invaded Belgium to attack the French, which prompted the United Kingdom to declare war on Germany. During the following years, Bulgaria and the Ottoman Empire would join Germany and Austria-Hungary as a part of the Central Powers, while Italy and the United States would add their lots in with the Allies.

The initial clashes involving huge conscript armies led to devastating casualties at battles such as Mons, the Marne, Tannenberg, Lemberg, and Ypres. By the end of 1914, a stalemate had ensued, with fortified lines of trenches, manned by millions of troops, running from the North Sea to the Swiss border in the West, and from the Baltic Sea to the Romanian border in the East.

Deadlock

New technologies had changed the face of warfare and left the generals of both sides in a difficult position. Machine guns, magazine rifles, quick firing artillery, high explosive shells, and barbed wire had altered the traditional battlefield, while the industrial capacity of the modern world meant that vast armies could be supplied and sustained for years on end. From late 1914 through to 1917, the commanders grappled with the challenges that these developments provided.

New Technology and Tactics

Innovative equipment and tactics were devised to break the deadlock. In 1915, the Germans introduced poison gas onto the battlefield but, despite some initial success, countermeasures were soon put in place to reduce its impact. In 1916, the British used the first tanks at the battle of the Somme. These were mechanically unreliable and painfully slow but showed some positive signs for the future. Artillery tactics were changed, moving from week-long bombardments to accurate counter-battery and interdiction fire. Creeping barrages were developed that advanced in front of infantry moving to assault enemy positions. Infantry tactics were also changed, arming men with more squad automatic weapons and hand grenades, and working in small groups to fight their way forward using infiltration.

In November 1917 at Cambrai, the British launched a short, devastating bombardment and advanced with tanks employed enmasse. The German line broke, but the British did not have the reserves ready to exploit their success. A quick German counterattack, preceded by an intense bombardment and new *Stosstruppen* (stormtroopers) units, recaptured much of the lost ground. The future of warfare had been revealed.

1918

The year 1918 opened with the Central Powers in their most favourable position since the beginning of the Great War. On the Eastern Front, Russia was defeated and rapidly dissolving into civil war. In the South, the Central Powers drove back the Italians decisively at Caporetto. On the Western Front, the French army was plagued with wide-scale mutinies and the British were recuperating after an exhausting offensive at Ypres.

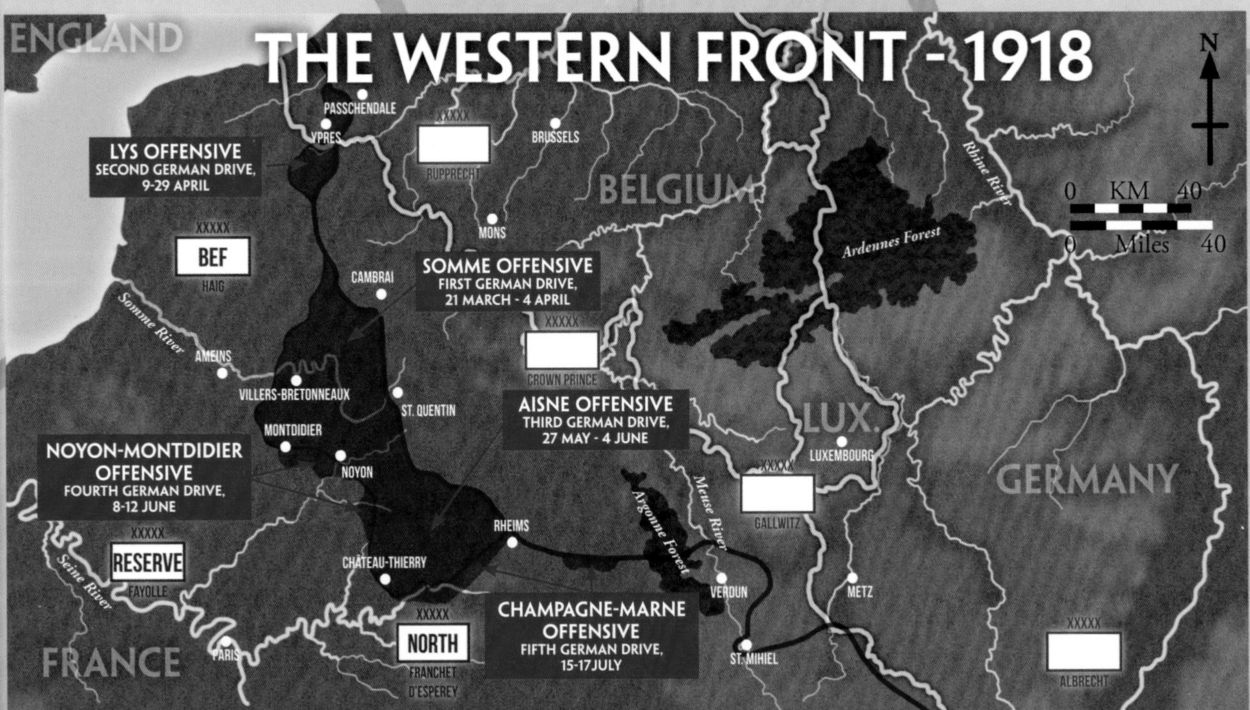

Meanwhile, veteran German units, flush with victories won on the Eastern Front, were transferring to the west to prepare for a grand spring offensive. It was imperative that the German Army attack soon as the Allied blockade was biting deep at home, and the slowly arriving US army would soon negate any advantages that the Germans possessed.

KAISERSCHLACHT

The battle was not long in coming. Convinced that the British Expeditionary Force (BEF) was his primary adversary, General Erich Ludendorff, commander of the Kaiser's army, aimed to drive the French and British apart by attacking around the Somme where the two Allied armies met. Operation Michael, the first attack in what would become known as the *Kaiserschlacht* (Emperor's Battle), opened on 21 March 1918.

Elite *Stosstruppen* infiltrated the British lines aided by a heavy morning fog, while follow-up troops neutralised redoubts. The British Fifth Army, having only recently taken over their line from the French and with their defences unfinished, buckled under the pressure. The first day of the offensive brought an unparalleled success to the German army, but at a high cost amounting to some 40,000 men.

The success of the German offensive prompted the Allies to appoint an overall commander, the French Field Marshall Ferdinand Foch. This effectively defeated the German objective of dividing the British and French, and at the same time gave the Allies a unified strategic direction. Allied reinforcements were rushed to plug the gaps and by the beginning of April, Operation Michael ground to a halt.

Four days later, the Germans launched another offensive in the Ypres area against the BEF. Codenamed 'Georgette', this battle aimed to push the British back towards the English Channel and hopefully force them to evacuate. Despite some tense moments, the British line held.

Finally, in May, Ludendorff switched the direction of his attacks, and attacked the French army on the Aisne River. This assault broke through, and the German army reached the river Marne for the first time since 1914.

Time was running out for Germany to win the war as Allied resistance stiffened. By mid July, Ludendorff's offensives had cost the German army half a million casualties. Although the Germans had inflicted more losses on the Allies, the arrival of US troops in ever greater numbers was rapidly making up for this. Moreover, a good portion of the casualties had been sustained by the best German troops who had led the attacks.

ALLIED ATTACKS

The initiative on the Western Front now shifted to the Allies. On 18 July, the French launched the Second Battle of the Marne and pushed the German Army back from all of its May gains. This was followed by the British attack at Amiens in August. Finally, the Americans launched their first offensives around St Mihiel and in the Meuse-Argonne region, while the French pressed forward in Champagne.

The best of the German army was kept opposite the British, but they had no answer to the sophisticated attacking machine that the British Army had become. In September, the British Army broke through the *Siegfried Stellung*, known as the Hindenburg Line by the Allies. This imposing defensive position was taken surprisingly quickly, and the BEF advanced as far as Mons in Belgium, where they had first encountered the German Army in 1914.

THE END...

In the meantime, Germany's partners had fallen. Bulgaria surrendered on 29 September after a combined Allied army of Serbs, British, French, Italians and Greeks broke through on the Macedonian front. They were followed by the Ottoman Empire, who sign a peace agreement with the British on 30 October, and then Austria-Hungary on 3 November after the Italians had pushed them back into Dalmatia (in modern day Croatia). Germany, with its army defeated and facing strikes, mutinies, and hunger at home, asked for an armistice, which came into effect at the 11th hour of the 11th day of the 11th month, November 1918.

GREAT WAR RULES

Great War uses the following rules in addition to those found in the *Flames Of War* rulebook.

GREAT WAR TRENCH FIGHTING

Trenches are one of the most iconic features of the First World War. Trenches use all of the usual Entrenchment rules found in the rulebook (see page 215), with the following exceptions.

Crossing Trenches

Trenches are deep and sometimes wide, making them formidable obstacles for early tanks.

Great War Trenches are rated as Difficult Going for Tank teams trying to cross them.

Fields of Fire

By 1918, both sides had digging trenches down to a science. Guns were integrated into the trenches so that their fields of fire interlocked and were mutually supporting.

When shooting or conducting Defensive Fire, teams can shoot over other friendly Infantry and Man-packed Gun teams that are in a Trench, whether or not the teams in the Trench have fired.

GREAT WAR GUNS

HMG Bombardments

Machine-gun bombardments are a way of breaking up enemy advances across no-man's land or to help keep the defenders' heads down during attacks.

HMG teams can fire Bombardments. These are conducted in the same way as a normal Artillery Bombardment.

Since they have Anti-tank and Firepower ratings of '-', they cannot harm Armoured vehicles or teams in Bulletproof Cover, although they can still Pin Down target platoons with a Hit in the Bombardment.

Trench Guns

Trench guns and mortars are specially designed to give the infantry their own close-support artillery. They are small enough to fit in trenches and light enough to be carried forward to assist in the assault.

Trench Guns can enter, cross, and be deployed in Trenches as though they were Man-packed guns.

Trench Guns use a medium base and face the long edge, like Man-packed gun teams.

GREAT WAR TANKS

Great War tanks were the world's first battle tanks. They ranged from large landships to small turreted tanks, similar in form to those we use today. These original tanks operate slightly different in Great War *Flames Of War*.

MOVEMENT RULES

Slow and Steady

Tanks of the Great War were built to help the infantry breakthrough. With that accomplished, they escorted the infantry onto the objectives.

Tank teams may not Move At The Double.

When moving through Rough Terrain or Slow Going, Tank teams reduce their Movement Distance to 4"/10cm. The tank may still attempt to use the Push It rule to try and get a little more out of the engine, taking another Bogging Check if necessary.

Push It

WWI tanks were notoriously unreliable. This was due to poor terrain, bad visibility, and the rudimentary engineering of the tank itself. However, many tanks had engineers or experienced crews to help get the most out of their vehicles.

When a Tank team that is not Bogged Down or Bailed Out completes its normal movement, it may roll a Skill Test to try and push the engine for a little more speed.

- *If the Tank team passes the Skill Test, the crew pushes the tank a bit more and it may move a further 2"/5cm.*
- *Otherwise, the Tank team stops as normal.*

However, if you roll a 1 for this Skill Test, your tank suffers a mechanical break down. Landships immediately receive a Damage marker (see Landship Damage & Repair rules on page 7). All other tanks immediately become Bogged Down.

Reliable

The British Mark V tanks had a new and improved engine and were much less likely to breakdown crossing the battlefield to engage the enemy.

Reliable Tank teams may Re-roll failed Skill Test to Push It.

In addition, if they roll a 1 for the re-rolled Skill Test, your tank does not suffer a mechanical break down. The Tank team just stops as normal.

Very Wide Tracks

The British Mark V* tank was very long and could cross trenches and other deep obstacles with ease.

If a Tank team with Very Wide Tracks becomes Bogged Down while attempting to cross Rough Terrain, roll again. On a roll of 3+ the vehicle immediately frees itself and continues moving.

Rough Ride

The British Mark V* tank was very long so it could carry a section of troops as passengers. Unfortunately the ride was so unpleasant that most troops were left dazed and sick from the fumes after their ride and needed some time to recover.

In a Step in which Passenger teams dismount from a Mark V tank, their platoon is immediately Pinned Down.*

SHOOTING RULES

Tank Weapons

Great War tanks are festooned with machine-guns and heavy guns. The tank's slow and steady speed allows the gun crews to operate independently, engaging the enemy in all directions while constantly on the move.

Tank teams may fire all main guns and machine-guns at the same time, at either the same platoon or different enemy platoons. All weapons that may Shoot do so at their full ROF, even if they have moved.

Shooting at Tanks

Mobile targets are difficult to hit under the best conditions, but add to that the fog of war, limited vision, heavy or immobile gun platforms, and clever tank commanders using zig-zag tactics, and it becomes even more difficult.

Reduce ROF by half (as shown in the ROF When Moving Table on page 91 of the rulebook) when shooting at a Tank team that is not Bogged Down, Bailed, or Damaged, unless the shooting team is an Infantry or Man-packed Gun team.

If the shooting team's ROF is 1, whether because it is moving, Pinned Down, or has a ROF 1 weapon, add +1 to the score needed hit the Tank team instead.

One-man Turret

The French Renault FT-17 was an innovative light tank with a turret, mounting either a machine-gun or a 37mm gun. However, it was only a small turret where the commander of the tank had to command, load and fire the gun.

Any Tank team with a One-man Turret that moves adds +1 to the score required to hit when shooting with its turret Main Gun. Machine-guns do not suffer this penalty.

ASSAULT RULES

Self-defence Machine-guns

Many tanks, such as the mighty landships, are equipped with self-defence machine-guns that the drivers and other crew can use in an emergency.

A Self-defence MG may not shoot, it is purely defensive.

In assault combat, if a hit from an Infantry or Gun team is allocated to a Tank with an Self-defence MG, the team that scored the hit must take another Skill Test.

- *If they pass the second Skill Test, the assaulting team gets past the machine-gun to hit the Tank team and the Tank must take an Armour Save as normal.*
- *Otherwise, the machine-gun has stopped the assaulting team and they fail to score a hit against the Tank team.*

Damaged tanks may still use their Self-defence MGs, however Bailed Out tanks may not.

Tanks Breaking Off

Even if it's slow, the tank is practically invulnerable to infantry in close-combat.

If a Tank team that is not Damaged, Bogged Down, or Bailed Out Breaks Off from an Assault, the Tank team does not need to be more than 4"/10cm from enemy teams for the assault to end, and the tank is not captured.

LANDSHIPS

Many early tanks were designed as massive landships with main guns and machine-guns covering the tank in all four directions. In *Flames Of War*, some tanks are Landships and use the rules below in addition to the Great War Tanks rules on pages 4 and 5.

MOVEMENT

Landships that Bog Down

Landships can overcome obstacles through sheer force, however sometimes they can get hung up on terrain or fall into a crater.

When a Landship would become Bogged Down it is Damaged and receives a Damage marker instead.

ASSAULT

Mobile Fortress

The machine-gun firepower of landships makes them devastating at close-quarters.

Mobile Fortresses, such as Mark IV female and A7V tanks, roll two dice in Assaults due to their large number of machine-guns.

SHOOTING

Shooting at Landships

Landships can withstand a lot of punishment and still keep fighting.

If a Landship is Destroyed by Shooting or an Artillery Bombardment, the shooting team immediately takes a second Firepower Test:

- *If it passes, the Landship is Destroyed outright.*
- *Otherwise, it is Damaged rather than Destroyed. Place a Damage marker on the Landship.*

If a Landship that is already Damaged is Destroyed, it is Destroyed outright with no further tests.

If a Landship needs to take multiple saves from an enemy platoon's shooting, take each save in turn, applying the result before taking the next save.

Landships that are Bailed Out

When a landship is not destroyed outright by a hit, its large crew can defend themselves at the same time as repairing the damage to get it back into the fight.

When a Landship would become Bailed Out it is Damaged and receives a Damage marker instead.

LANDSHIP DAMAGE & REPAIR

Damaged Landships

Even while damaged, a landship is a dangerous beast.

A Landship that has one Damage marker cannot move, but can still shoot, and if assaulted, fight.

Damaged a Second Time

The design of a landship is rugged and difficult for the enemy to destroy in combat.

If a Landship that is Damaged becomes Damaged a second time, it gains a second Damage marker.

A Landship that has two Damage markers cannot move, shoot, or fight in assaults.

Damaged a Third Time

Landships are tough, but there is only so much a crew can take before they feel it may be safer somewhere away from their steel beast.

Each time a Landship that already has two Damage markers is Damaged again, take an immediate Motivation Test:

- *If the test is passed, the damage is superficial and has no effect on the tank (do not place a third Damage marker).*
- *If the test is failed, the crew decides that it's too dangerous to remain with their vehicle and it is Destroyed.*

Repairing Damaged Landships

Most landships have an engineer on board to deal with repairing damage and restarting stalled engines.

During the Starting Step at the start of your turn, roll a Skill Test for each Damage marker on each Landship:

- *If the test is successful, the crew repairs their vehicle. Remove the Damage marker.*
- *If the test fails, the crew is still struggling to get the tank working, and you'll have to wait until the start of your next turn to roll again.*

If all Damage markers are repaired the Landship can now act as normal this turn.

Damaged Landships in Assaults

With the crew distributed between different compartments, with little communication between them, the gunners often have little idea why the tank stopped, fighting on regardless.

In Assaults, a Landship that has one Damage marker:

- *is not ignored for Tank Terror and prevents the Assaulting Platoon from winning the Assault if within 4"/10cm.*

In Assaults, a Landship that has two Damage markers:

- *is ignored for Tank Terror and does not prevent the Assaulting Platoon from winning the Assault if within 4"/10cm.*

Damage Chart

Damage Tokens	Effect on the Landship			
Number of Markers	Move	Shoot	Launch an Assault	Fight in Assault
No Damage	✓	✓	✓	✓
1 Damage	✗	✓	✗	✓
2+ Damage	✗	✗	✗	✗

BRITISH TANK PROFILES

MARK IV, V, AND V* FEMALE TANK

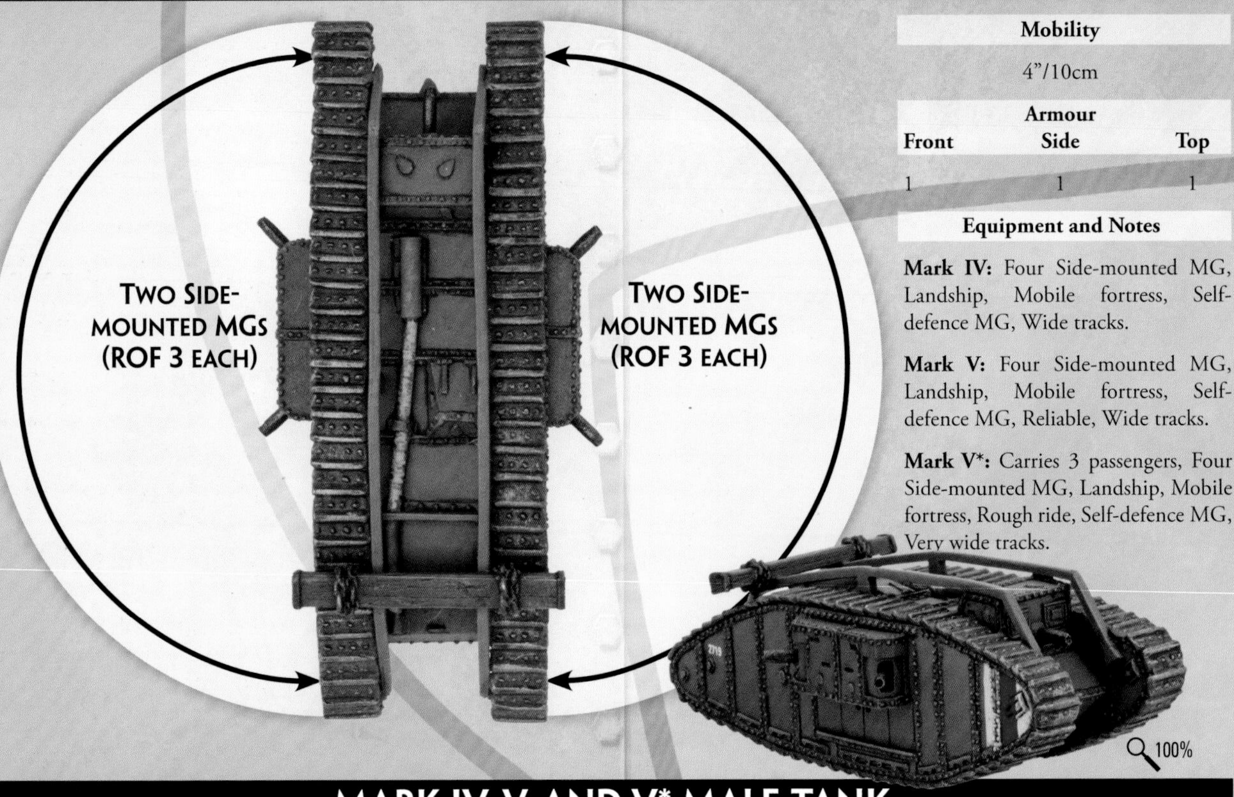

Mobility		
4"/10cm		

Armour		
Front	Side	Top
1	1	1

Equipment and Notes

Mark IV: Four Side-mounted MG, Landship, Mobile fortress, Self-defence MG, Wide tracks.

Mark V: Four Side-mounted MG, Landship, Mobile fortress, Self-defence MG, Reliable, Wide tracks.

Mark V*: Carries 3 passengers, Four Side-mounted MG, Landship, Mobile fortress, Rough ride, Self-defence MG, Very wide tracks.

100%

MARK IV, V, AND V* MALE TANK

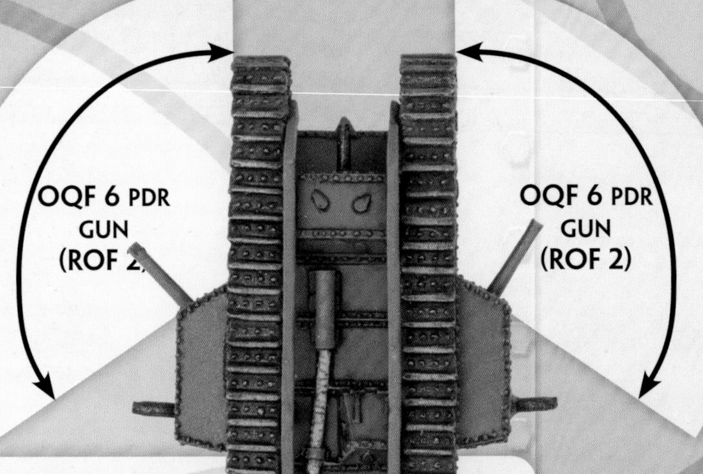

Mobility		
4"/10cm		

Armour		
Front	Side	Top
1	1	1

Equipment and Notes

Mark IV: Landship, Self-defence MG, Wide tracks.

Mark V: Landship, Self-defence MG, Reliable, Wide tracks.

Mark V*: Carries 3 passengers, Landship, Rough ride, Self-defence MG, Very wide tracks.

The Mark IV male tank had three Lewis machine-guns for self-defence. When enemy infantry got in too close, the driver would man the Lewis mounted in the drivers' compartment and the OQF 6 pdr gunners took up the ones mounted in the sponsons. Once the threat was dealt with, the crew returned to their posts and fought on.

The Mark V and Mark V tanks improved on this by adding a rear-mounted machine-gun for self-defence. In additional the Mark V and Mark V* tanks used Hotchkiss machine-guns instead of Lewis machine-guns.*

OQF 6 PDR GUN

Range		
24"/60cm		

ROF	Anti-tank	Firepower
2	6	4+

Equipment and Notes

Side mounted.

100%

MARK V, AND V* HERMAPHRODITE TANK

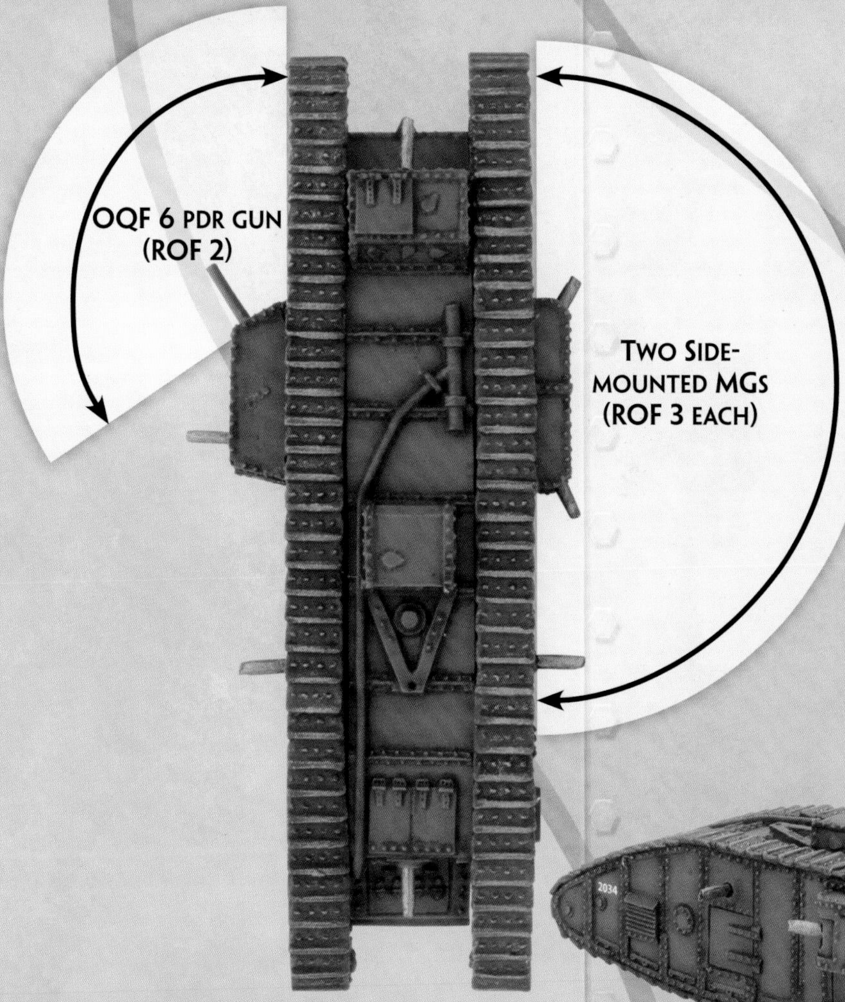

OQF 6 PDR GUN (ROF 2)

TWO SIDE-MOUNTED MGS (ROF 3 EACH)

Mobility		
4"/10cm		
Armour		
Front	**Side**	**Top**
1	1	1

Equipment and Notes

Mark V: Two Side-mounted MG, Landship, Self-defence MG, Reliable, Wide tracks.

Mark V*: Carries 3 passengers, Two Side-mounted MG Landship, Rough ride, Self-defence MG, Very wide tracks

OQF 6 PDR GUN

Range		
24"/60cm		
ROF	**Anti-tank**	**Firepower**
2	6	4+

Equipment and Notes

Side mounted.

100%

The Mark V and Mark V hermaphrodite tanks were a hybrid of the male and female variant, with a gun sponson on one hull side and a machine-gun sponson on the opposite hull side.*

MEDIUM TANK MARK A WHIPPET

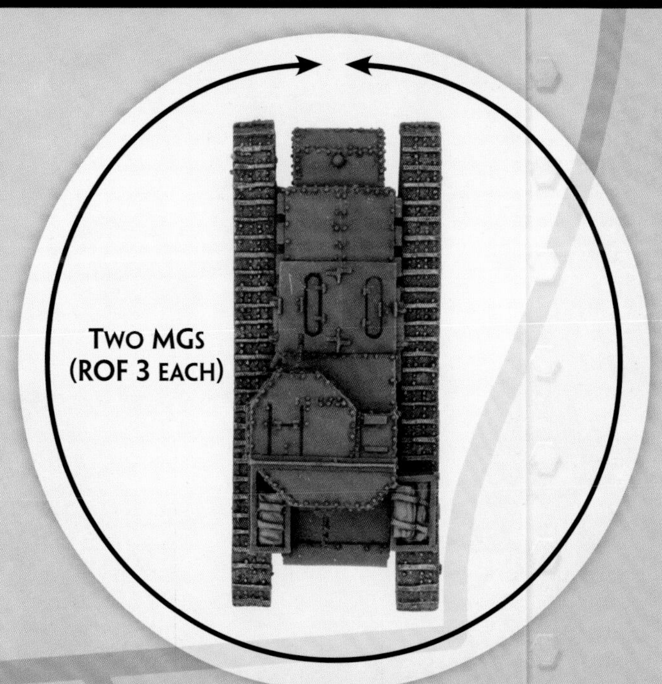

Mobility		
8"/20cm		
Armour		
Front	**Side**	**Top**
1	1	1

Equipment and Notes

Two MG.

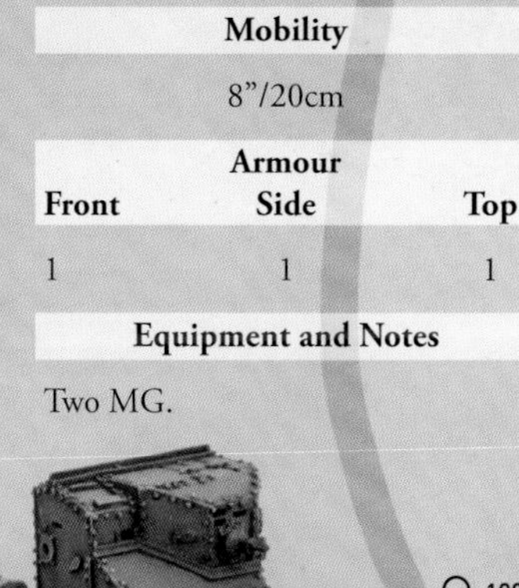

100%

GERMAN TANK PROFILE

A7V TANK

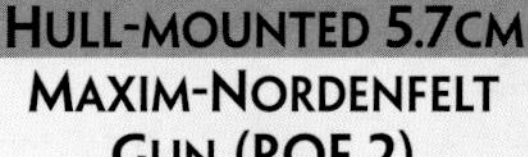

HULL-MOUNTED 5.7CM MAXIM-NORDENFELT GUN (ROF 2)

TWO SIDE-MOUNTED MGS (ROF 3 EACH)

TWO SIDE-MOUNTED MGS (ROF 3 EACH)

TWO REAR-MOUNTED MGS (ROF 3 EACH)

Mobility		
6"/15cm		
Armour		
Front	Side	Top
2	1	1

Equipment and Notes

Four Side-mounted MG, Two hull-rear MG, Landship, Mobile fortress, Overloaded, Self-defence MG.

5.7CM MAXIM-NORDENFELT GUN

Range		
24"/60cm		
ROF	Anti-tank	Firepower
2	6	4+

Equipment and Notes

Hull mounted.

FRENCH TANK PROFILES

RENAULT FT-17

TURRET MG (ROF 3) OR 37MM SA-18 GUN (ROF 2)

Mobility		
8"/20cm		
Armour		
Front	Side	Top
1	1	1

Equipment and Notes

Turret MG or 37mm SA-18 gun.

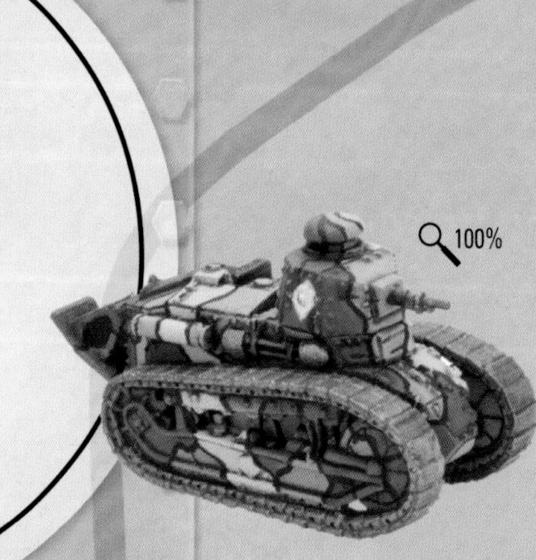

37MM SA-18 GUN

Range		
16"/40cm		
ROF	Anti-tank	Firepower
2	4	4+

Equipment and Notes

One-man turret.

SCHNEIDER CA.1

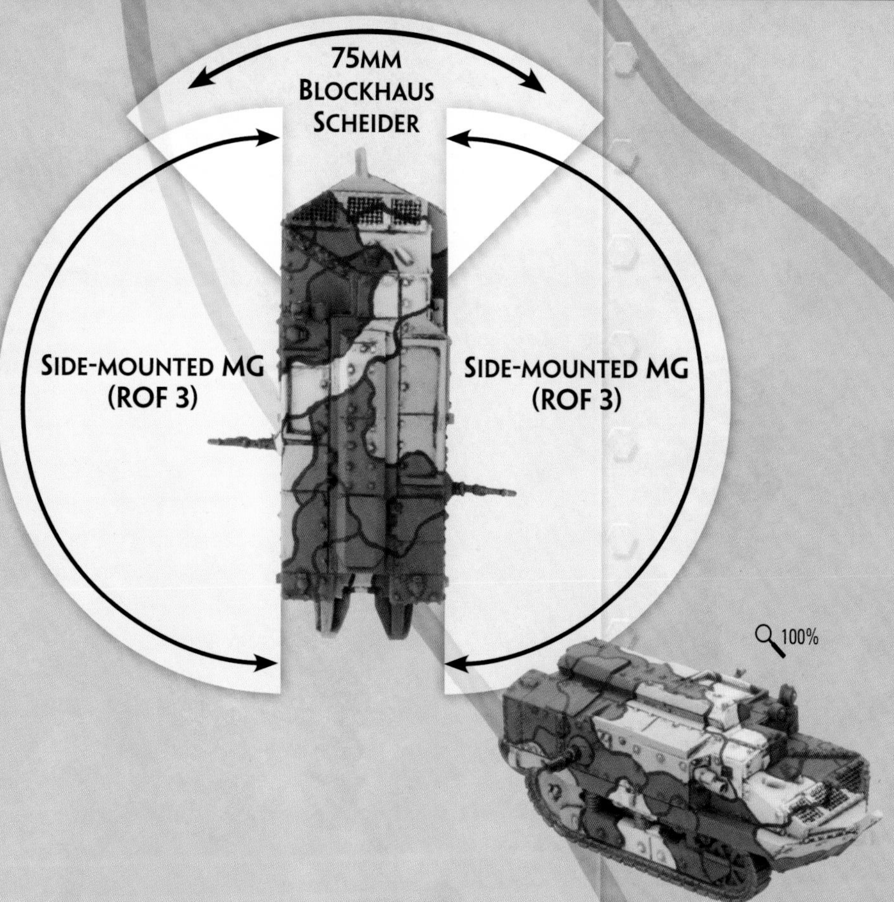

Mobility		
4"/10cm		
Armour		
Front	Side	Top
1	1	1
Equipment and Notes		

Two side-mounted MG, Landship, Overloaded.

75MM BLOCKHAUS SCHEIDER

Range		
16"/40cm		
ROF	Anti-tank	Firepower
2	5	3+
Equipment and Notes		

Side mounted.

CHAR SAINT CHAMOND

Hull-mounted 75mm mle 1897 gun (ROF 2) Hull MG (ROF 3)

Side-mounted MG (ROF 3)

Side-mounted MG (ROF 3)

Hull-rear MG (ROF 3)

100%

Mobility		
4"/10cm		
Armour		
Front	Side	Top
1	1	1
Equipment and Notes		

Hull MG, Two side-mounted MG, Hull-rear MG, Landship, Overloaded.

75MM MLE 1897 GUN

Range		
24"/60cm		
ROF	Anti-tank	Firepower
2	8	3+
Equipment and Notes		

Hull mounted.

PANZERS GO TO WAR
VILLERS-BRETONNEUX, 1918

In late April 1918, Ludendorff was ready to resume the offensive with Amiens as the main objective. The key to this town was a small village positioned on the high ground above Amiens, called Villers-Bretonneux. The main effort of the German offensive against Amiens was directed at Villers-Bretonneux. The attack was led by three units of A7V tanks, known as *Sturm-Panzerkraftwagen Abteilung 1, 2,* and *3* (or ATD 1, ATD 2, and ATD 3) totalling 13 tanks. Each ATD was paired with an assault division and assigned three objectives around Villers-Bretonneux.

The village itself was positioned in no-man's-land and had been lost to the British earlier in the Spring offensive. Anticipating the attack, the British assembled a force, including troops and tanks, to recapture it.

On the morning of 24 April 1918, the Germans opened fire with a preliminary bombardment, including gas attacks against the British artillery and reserve assembly areas. The bombardment succeeded in suppressing the enemy as the A7Vs trundled forward followed closely by *Stosstruppen* (shock troops) and regular infantry. Scores of British POWs were rounded up east of the town as the Germans advanced.

A thick fog helped the Germans advance on the British 8th Division, and soon the A7Vs were deep into enemy lines. The British had little answer to the German tanks that pressed on without remorse.

Armoured Face Off

In concert with the infantry, the A7Vs of ATD 2 overcame their initial objectives and continued toward the main British line. As they neared, three British Mark IV tanks, two females and a male, approached and opened fire with machine-guns and 6-pdr guns. The lead A7V, *Nixe* (Mermaid), spotted the British tanks and quickly returned fire. The result was devastating as the A7V tore huge holes through the two female tanks with its 57mm main gun.

As the female tanks limped away, *Nixe* pressed on believing it had destroyed all three tanks. However, the male tank remained, using dips in the ground as cover and returning fire. After several near misses, the Mark IV landed three solid hits on *Nixe*. The German tank halted and the crew bailed out. The timely arrival of the A7Vs *Siegfried* and *Schnuck* forced the Mark IV to retire.

Moments later, the British sent forward seven Mark A Medium tanks, known as Whippets. These fast tanks were running amok through the German infantry left on its own as the A7Vs manoeuvred to battle the Mark IVs. *Siegfried* was in a good position to help and quickly knocked out two of the Whippets with its 57mm gun, putting an end to the British tank charge.

The Whippets retreated into the sights of *Schnuck*, which had arrived on the scene. The A7V knocked out another medium tank as did a German 77mm field gun. The three remaining Whippets limped back to the British lines.

By 1545 hours, the German attack had lost forward momentum as British heavy machine-guns stopped the German infantry. Without an assault to support, the A7Vs retired, and the fighting was over for the time being.

That evening, under the cover of darkness, an Australian counterattack finally recaptured Villers-Bretonneux, ending the German offensive against Amiens.

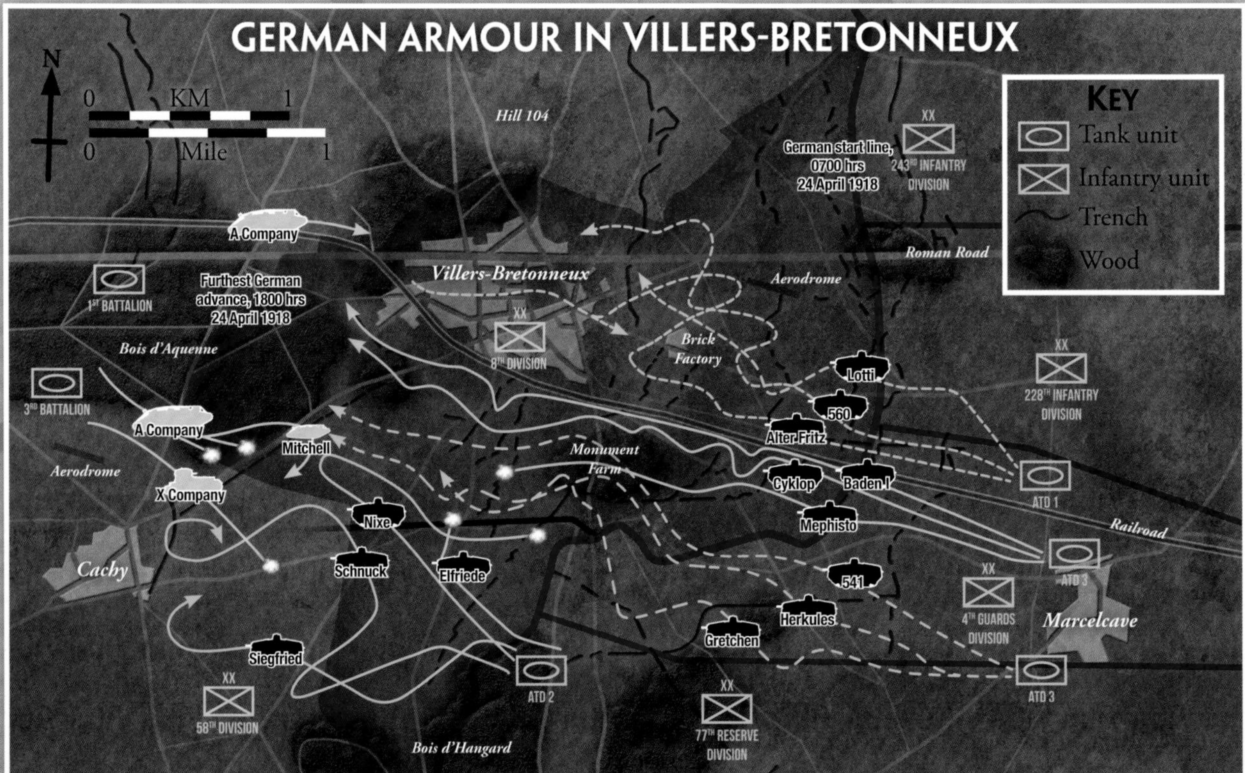

German Panzers at Villers-Bretonneux

Sturm-Panzerkraftwagen Abteilung 1

Abteilung 1 (or ATD 1) had seen combat earlier than Villers-Bretonneux, but their crews were still trying to come to grips with the new technology. The Abteilung was assigned to the 228th Infantry Division for the attack.

Sturm-Panzerkraftwagen Abteilung 2

Abteilung 2 (or ATD 2) was about to test their machines and engage in history's first tank versus tank duel. The Abteilung was assigned to the 77th Reserve Division for the attack.

Sturm-Panzerkraftwagen Abteilung 3

Abteilung 3 (or ATD 3) used the highest number of A7V tanks at Villers-Bretonneux. The Abteilung was assigned to the elite 4th Guards Infantry Division for the attack.

German Special Rules

A German Infanteriekompanie does not use any of the German special rules found in the* Flames Of War *rulebook, and instead uses the following special rule.

Infantrie Vor!

The German army is exceptionally well equipped with the latest technologies and tactics in warfare. The first major use of *Stosstactik* (or Storm Tactics) was at Capretto in 1917, where the Germans successfully infiltrated and decisively defeated the Italians in north-eastern Italy. Following this victory, the *Stoss* troops were divided among the western divisions to teach their tactics and spread the word about infiltration tactics.

Historically, German troops have always been more aggressive and flexible than their opponents in order to gain major advantages. This, added with the new *Stoss* tactics, has given the German soldier an edge in combat. Quickly closing with the enemy means less time that they have to spend under enemy fire. All troops, from the regular infantryman to the elite stormtrooper, use rapid advance and tactical flexibility to take advantage of enemy weaknesses quickly and decisively.

Any German platoon with a Platoon Command team may attempt an Infantrie Vor! move in its Assault Step. Tank teams cannot make Infantrie Vor! moves.

Roll a Skill Test for each platoon:

- *If the test is passed, the platoon treats the Assault Step as a Movement Step in which it can move up to another 4"/10cm, regardless of its normal movement distance.*
- *If the test is failed, the platoon cannot move any further this turn.*

Either way, a platoon that attempts to make an Infantrie Vor! move cannot take any part in an assault in the same turn.

Although it is not the Movement Step, teams making an Infantrie Vor! move may Mount and Dismount as if it was the Movement Step.

Platoons that are Pinned Down or have moved At the Double, and teams that are Bogged Down, cannot make Infantrie Vor! moves.

Immobile Gun teams and Gun teams that shot earlier in the turn cannot make an Infantrie Vor! move. Teams of any type that have fired an Artillery Bombardment cannot make an Infantrie Vor! move.

Infanteriekompanie

(Infantry Company)

Infantry Company

You must field one platoon from each box shaded black and may field one platoon from each box shaded grey.

Your Company HQ must be either from a Reserve division (marked ◉), or an Infantry division (marked ✠). All other platoons with any of these symbols must be from the same division as your Company HQ.

SUPPORT PLATOONS

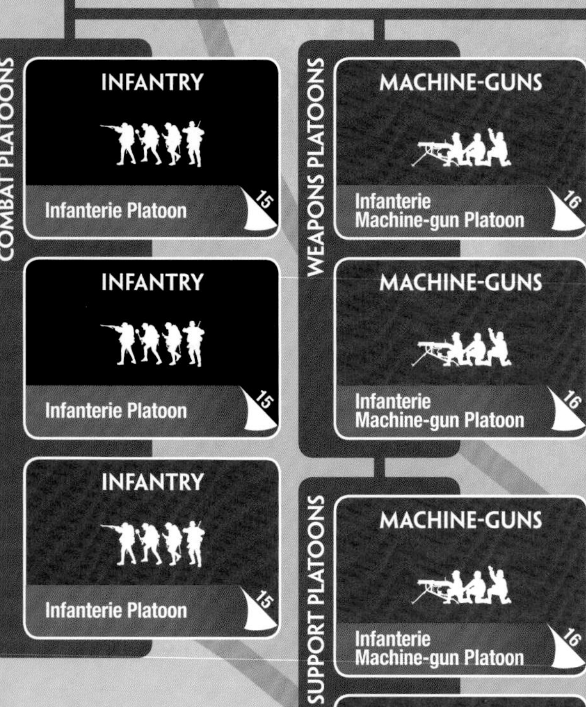

Motivation and Skill

Reserve divisions are fresh units and are rated **Confident Trained**.

Infantry divisions have seen a lot of combat recently and are rated **Confident Veteran**.

Reserve Division	
RELUCTANT	CONSCRIPT
CONFIDENT	**TRAINED**
FEARLESS	VETERAN

Infantry Division	
RELUCTANT	CONSCRIPT
CONFIDENT	TRAINED
FEARLESS	**VETERAN**

HEADQUARTERS

Infanteriekompanie HQ

Headquarters

	Reserve	Infantry
Company HQ	25 points	30 points

Add Anti-tank Rifle Section with:

3 Anti-tank Rifle teams	135 points	180 points
2 Anti-tank Rifle teams	90 points	120 points
1 Anti-tank Rifle team	45 points	60 points

Add Flame-thrower Section with:

3 Flame-thrower teams	90 points	120 points
2 Flame-thrower teams	60 points	80 points
1 Flame-thrower team	30 points	40 points

Add Werfer Section with:

2 Granatenwerfer teams	90 points	120 points
1 Granatenwerfer team	45 points	60 points

Options

- Replace Command Pistol teams with Command SMG teams for +5 points per team.
- Add up to one Sniper team for +60 points.

Excellent German technology has given us the tools we need to overcome the enemy tanks and trenches, including powerful anti-tank rifles, devastating flame-throwers, and more.

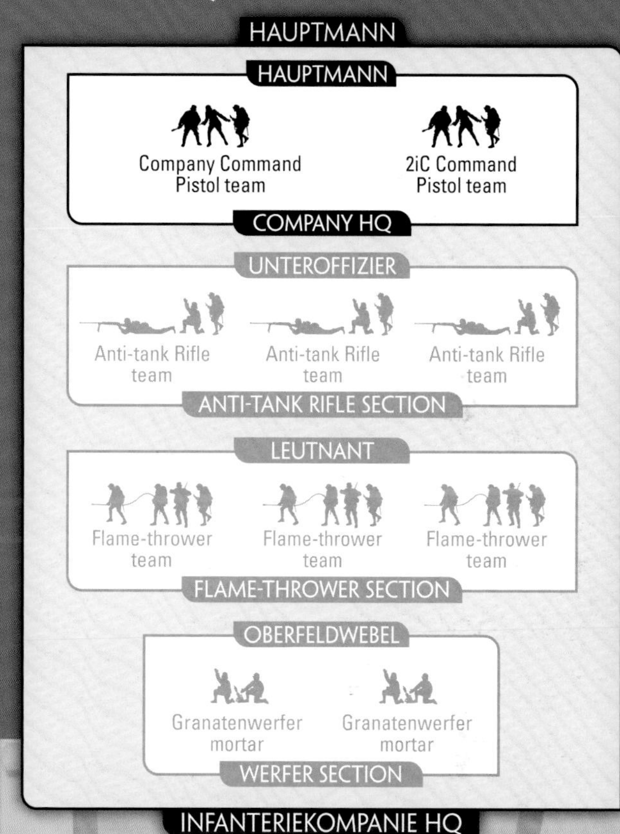

COMBAT PLATOONS

Infanterie Platoon

Platoon

HQ Section with:

	Reserve	Infantry
2 Rifle Squads and 2 Machine-gun Squads	150 points	195 points
2 Rifle Squads and 1 Machine-gun Squad	110 points	145 points

Options

- Replace Command Pistol team with a Command SMG team for +5 points.
- Replace up to one Rifle team with a Rifle Grenade team for +5 points.

The steadfast infantryman has been fighting this war for years. However, he is not alone. With tanks, stormtroopers, and special trench guns to help, the rifleman will claim victory.

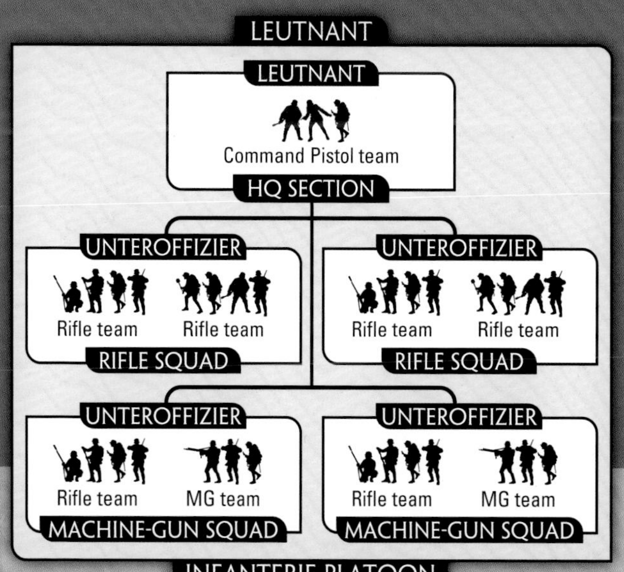

WEAPONS PLATOONS

Infanterie Machine-gun Platoon

Platoon

HQ Section with:		
4 Maxim HMG	285 points	370 points
3 Maxim HMG	215 points	280 points
2 Maxim HMG	145 points	190 points

German Maxim HMG teams have an Anti-tank rating of 3 due to the use of armour-piercing ammunition.

In addition, an Infantrie Machine-gun Platoon may fire bombardments (see page 4).

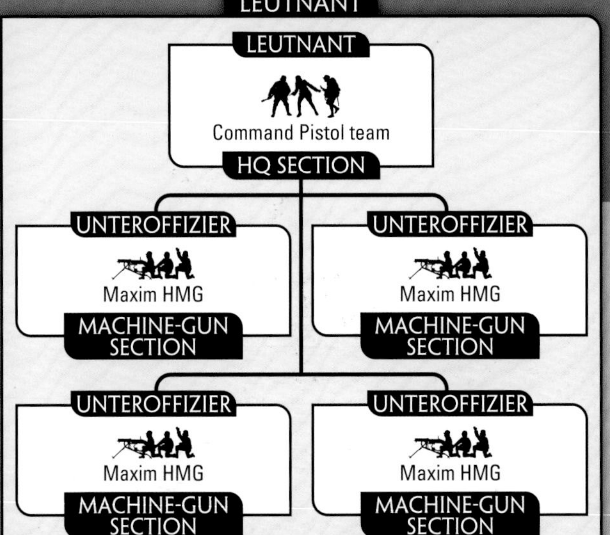

The Maxim machine-gun has drastically changed how battles are fought. Now a small crew of men can put out a remarkable amount of fire. Multiply this across a whole platoon of these weapons and you have a unit capable of an immense rate of fire.

REGIMENTAL SUPPORT PLATOONS

Minenwerfer Platoon

Platoon

3 7.6cm Minenwerfer	390 points	510 points
2 7.6cm Minenwerfer	260 points	340 points
1 7.6cm Minenwerfer	130 points	170 points

Minenwefer Sections operate as separate platoons, each gun is their own Command team.

7.6cm Minenwerfer gun teams are Trench Guns (see page 4).

LEUTNANT
LEUTNANT
Command 7.6cm Minenwerfer mortar
MINENWERFER SECTION
UNTEROFFIZIER
Command 7.6cm Minenwerfer mortar
MINENWERFER SECTION
UNTEROFFIZIER
Command 7.6cm Minenwerfer mortar
MINENWERFER SECTION
MINENWERFER PLATOON

Infantry alone lack the firepower to dig out enemy troops and fortifications. To address this problem the German army employs the *Minenwerfer* (mine-thrower or mortar). Its high explosive shells are essential for knocking out enemy strong points. When enemy tanks are about, the Minenwerfer can be used to combat these beasts in an anti-tank role.

Anti-tank Gun Platoon

Platoon	◎	✠
2 3.7cm TaK	170 points	220 points
1 3.7cm TaK	85 points	110 points

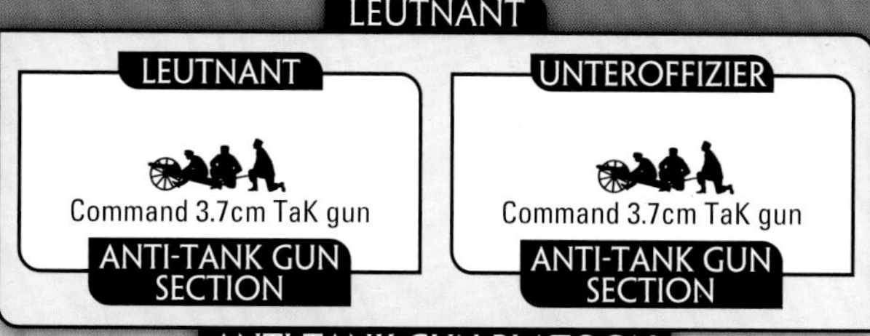

Anti-tank Gun Sections operate as separate platoons, each gun is their own Command team.

With enemy tanks on the prowl, the German army has developed several weapons to deal with them. One of these is the relatively light-weight 3.7cm TaK gun, built by Rheinmetall. It has the ability to penetrate enemy tanks' armour and knock them out. It's low profile also makes it suitable to move across no-man's-land to support the infantry.

SUPPORT PLATOONS

Panzer Platoon

Platoon	✠
3 A7V	855 points
2 A7V	570 points
1 A7V	285 points
3 Beute Mk IV female	690 points
2 Beute Mk IV female	460 points
1 Beute Mk IV female	230 points

Options

- Replace any or all Beute Mk IV female tanks with Beute Mk IV male tanks for +30 points per tank.
- Replace any or all A7V tanks with Beute Mk IV female for -55 points or Beute Mk IV male tanks for -25 points per tank.

HAUPTMANN

HAUPTMANN

Command Panzer

HQ SECTION

LEUTNANT

Command Panzer

PANZER SECTION

LEUTNANT

Command Panzer

PANZER SECTION

PANZER PLATOON

Panzer Sections operate as separate platoons, each tank is their own Command team.

An Infanteriekompanie that includes a Panzer Platoon will Always Attack, unless it also includes an Artillery Battery, which will make it Always Defend.

A Panzer Platoon is rated **Confident Trained.**

CONFIDENT	TRAINED

We have created our own panzers. Bristling with machine guns and a 57mm gun, the A7V is an impressive weapon with thicker armour and faster mobility than most enemy tanks. In addition, we use captured enemy tanks to take the fight back to their original owners.

Infantry Gun Platoon

Platoon

2 7.62cm Krupp IG	210 points	270 points
1 7.62cm Krupp IG	105 points	135 points

LEUTNANT

LEUTNANT — Command Infantry gun — INFANTRY GUN SECTION

UNTEROFFIZIER — Command Infantry gun — INFANTRY GUN SECTION

INFANTRY GUN PLATOON

Infantry Gun Sections operate as separate platoons, each gun is their own Command team.

7.62cm Krupp IG gun teams are Trench Guns (see page 4).

The 7.62cm Krupp infantry gun has outstanding accuracy and is lightweight, making it a favourite among the crews that use it. It gives German infantry a weapon capable of destroying the targets that heavy artillery misses or attacking enemy tanks. This makes it a very versatile and essential part of an assault.

Artillery Battery

Platoon

HQ Section with:

4 7.7cm FK96 n.A.	545 points	710 points
2 7.7cm FK96 n.A.	275 points	360 points

Option

- Add horse-drawn limbers for +5 points for the battery.

An Infanteriekompanie that includes an Artillery Battery will Always Defend.

The armies of this Great War rely heavily on artillery to help prepare the enemy for an assault or to break up enemy attacks. The 7.7cm FK96 n.A. is a versatile field gun used all across the front. Its light weight makes it a very mobile gun compared to its competitors. With a variety of shells available, ranging from anti-tank to shrapnel rounds, this gun can be employed successfully in different combat situations. This gives commanders a valuable tool in both offensive and defensive operations.

Artillery Detachment

Platoon

2 7.7cm FK96 n.A.	260 points	340 points
1 7.7cm FK96 n.A.	130 points	170 points

Option

- Add horse-drawn limbers for +5 points for the battery.

LEUTNANT

LEUTNANT — Command 7.7cm FK96 n.A. gun — Horse-drawn limber — GUN SECTION

UNTEROFFIZER — Command 7.7cm FK96 n.A. gun — Horse-drawn limber — GUN SECTION

ARTILLERY DETACHMENT

Gun Sections operate as separate platoons, each gun is their own Command team.

The 7.7cm FK96 n.A. is relatively light enough to be useful as a rapid-response anti-tank detachment. Held just behind the lines in reserve, these guns can be called up to meet enemy tanks. The gun is powerful and remains the best way to take out a tank permanently, but it can also be used to knock out enemy bunkers or gun positions.

STOSSTAKTIK

When the war stagnated into trench warfare, officers on both sides tried to break the stalemate. Various new weapons were tried: massed heavy artillery bombardments, poison gas, aircraft, and tanks. Yet the most effective change was not a new weapon, but a new tactic. A revolution in military thinking occurred, with the strict discipline and drill that had been required of infantry since the days of Frederick the Great giving way to newer, more flexible movement and tactics.

In the German army these tactics were called *Stosstaktik,* or shock tactics. They were to be carried out by *Stosstruppen* (shock troops). The aim of the *Stosstruppen* was to seek out weak points in the enemy lines and advance through them quickly in small groups. Enemy strongpoints would be bypassed in order to capture objectives in their rear.

Shock tactics were first conceived in 1915 by *Hauptmann* (Captain) Willy Rohr, a career infantry officer. He realized that current assault tactics did not work. He reorganized his assault detachment into squad-sized assault groups, teaching them to move quickly and quietly using cover. Enemy trenches were rolled up in short rushes with grenades. The new tactics were tested in the Vosges Mountains, and they worked well.

Rohr began training more men in his tactics and the detachment was expanded into *Sturmbatallion Rohr* (Assault Battalion Rohr). The battalion took part in the initial attack at Verdun in 1916, successfully clearing the first line of French trenches.

Rohr's idea was adopted by his commander, Eighth Army General Hutier. Hutier added a short, sharp artillery bombardment before the assault. This would silence defenders and achieve tactical surprise. Detailed planning was reduced, and junior officers would be given more freedom to adapt tactics to the situation.

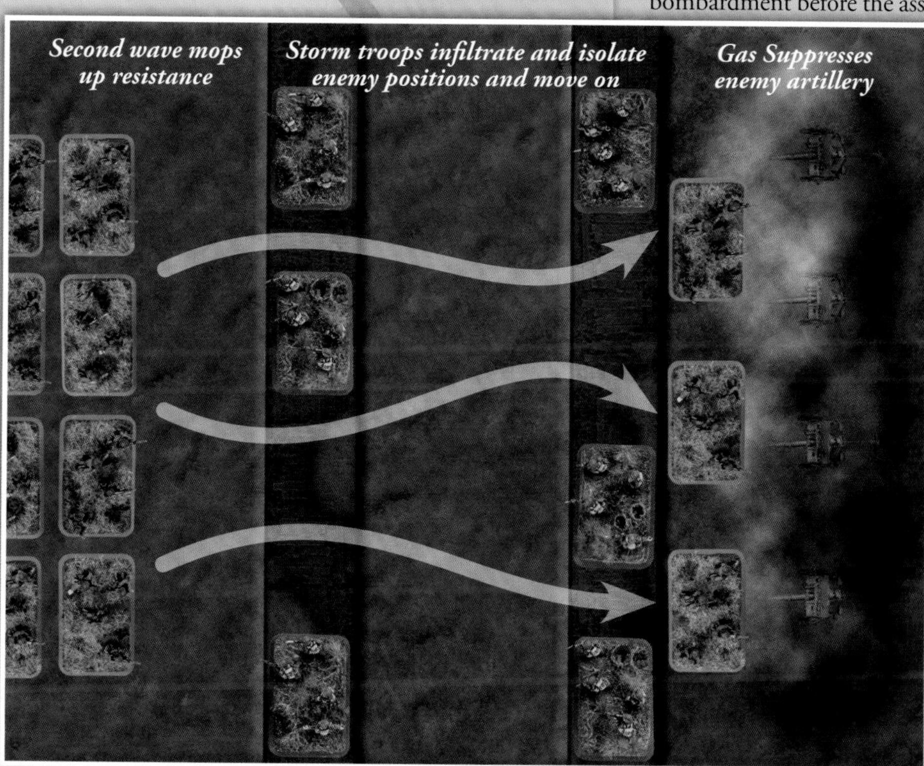

Through 1917, the new tactics continued to be used and adapted successfully. New units of *Stosstruppen* were raised and distributed across the front for major assaults.

Stosstaktik was used on a large scale during the 1918 Spring offensive. Entire divisions infiltrated and quickly overran the French and British trench lines, ending the stalemate that had lasted four years. Generals Hindenburg and Ludendorff are usually given the credit for planning this offensive, but none of it could have happened without Willy Rohr's new idea.

STOSSTAKTIK SPECIAL RULES

TRENCH FIGHTERS

Few soldiers had the experience and skill in hand-to-hand combat as German *Stosstruppen.*

SMG and Pistol teams from a Stoss Platoon hit on a roll of 2+ in Assaults (instead of 3+).

STOSSTRUPPEN INFILTRATION

Stosstruppen tactics relied on infiltration to close with the enemy undetected. Once in position, the assault troops were ready to unleash hell on the enemy trenches.

If you are the Attacker and have deployed at least one Stoss Platoon on the table, then all of the Stoss and Infanterie Platoons in your force may make a Spearhead Deployment move (see page 261 of the rulebook).

MISSION TACTICS

Before battle, every stormtrooper is briefed on their mission and how it relates to the overall battle plan.

If a Stoss Platoon's Command team is Destroyed, another team takes over immediately. Remove any other Infantry team in the platoon that is within Command Distance of the Command team and replace it with the original Platoon Command team.

If there is no Infantry team within Command Distance, then the Platoon Command team is Destroyed and the platoon is left leaderless.

The original Platoon Command team can still use this rule while a Warrior team is leading the platoon and acting as its Command team, but the rule does not apply to the Warrior team.

Stosskompanie

(Assault Company)

Infantry Company

You must field one platoon from each box shaded black and may field one platoon from each box shaded grey.

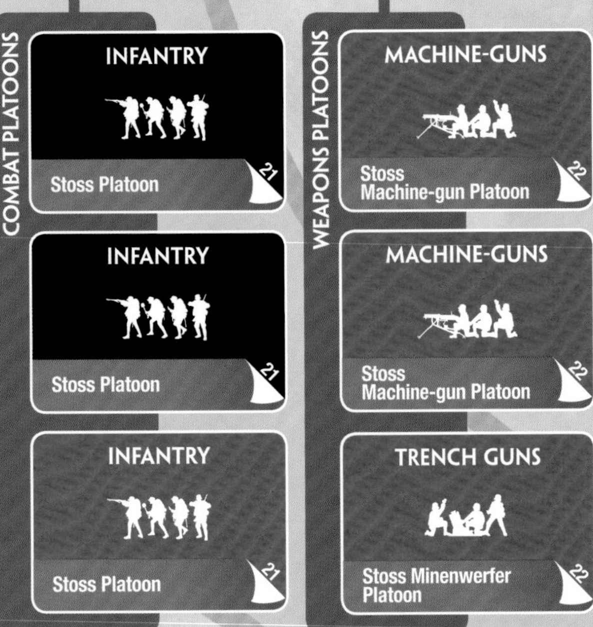

STOSSKOMPANIE SPECIAL RULES

A German Stosskompanie does not use any of the German special rules found in the Flames Of War rulebook, and instead uses the Infantrie Vor! special rule on page 13, Trench Fighters, Stosstruppen Infiltration, and Mission Tactics special rules on page 19, and the Night Attack special rule below.

Night Attack

Stosstruppen were experts of infiltration and were able to locate and bypass enemy strong points. They often did not use an artillery bombardment to soften up the enemies defences, instead using the night and the terrain to sneak past the enemy.

A player commanding a Stosskompanie may elect to make a Night Attack in missions that do not use the Meeting Engagement special rule (see age 264 of the rulebook). If they do so, the game starts at night and uses the Dawn rules on page 273 of the rulebook. If the German player elects to Night Attack, the Mission does not use the Preliminary Bombardment mission special rule.

STOSSTRUPPEN

Developed as a response to trench warfare, *Stosstruppen* (Assault Troops) were trained in the use of infiltration tactics combined with speed and mobility in order to move past enemy strongpoints and attack rear areas such as supply dumps, headquarters, and artillery emplacements. While the *Stoss* may be most identified with the German offensives made in 1918, the concept was developed much earlier in the war.

In an attack, the *Stosskompanie* would move out in front of the main body of troops and bypass enemy strong points that were left for regular troops to contend with. Once in the enemy's rear area, *Stosstruppen* would create mayhem, disrupting communications and preventing the enemy from mounting a counter attack.

Motivation and Skill

A number of well-preforming units were selected for special training in the new Stosstaktik (Assault Tactics) from 1915. These units were then used to spread training of these new tactics throughout the German Army. Eventually, most divisions had at least one kompanie of these specialists. A Sturm Battalion Stosskompanie is rated as **Fearless Veteran.**

RELUCTANT	CONSCRIPT
CONFIDENT	TRAINED
FEARLESS	**VETERAN**

HEADQUARTERS

Stosskompanie HQ

Headquarters

Company HQ	35 points

- Replace either or both Command Pistol teams with Command SMG teams for +5 points per team.

Add Flame-thrower Section with:

3 Flame-thrower teams	150 points
2 Flame-thrower teams	100 points
1 Flame-thrower team	50 points

Option

- Add up to one Sniper team for +60 points.

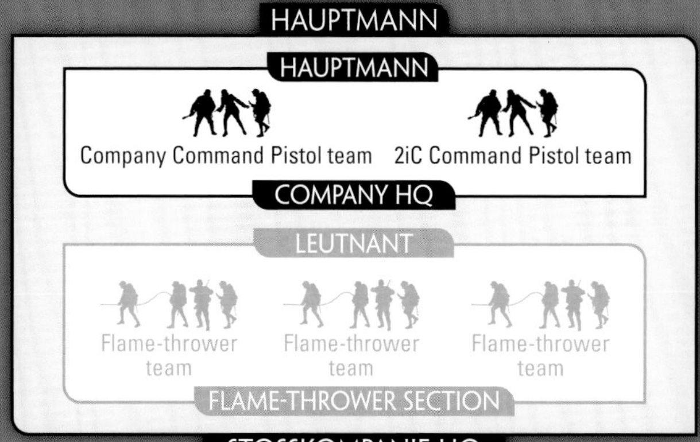

Our *Stosskompanie* uses the latest tactics to get past the enemies front line and cause havoc in their rear areas. We will travel lighter than our infantry counter parts and when the opportunity is right we will close in and finish them off with a furious assault. Coming up behind us is our supporting infantry, heavy weapons, and armour to deal with what we leave in our wake.

COMBAT PLATOONS

Stoss Platoon

Platoon

HQ Section with:

2 Sturm Squads and 2 Machine-gun Squads	305 points
2 Sturm Squads and 1 Machine-gun Squad	240 points

Options

- Replace Command Pistol team with a Command SMG team for +5 points.
- Add a Flame-thrower team for +50 points.

A Stoss Platoon uses the Stosstactik special rules on page 19.

Pistol and SMG teams in a Stoss Platoon are rated Tank Assault 3.

An Infanteriekompanie that includes a Stoss Platoon will Always Attack, unless it also includes an Artillery Battery, which will make it Always Defend.

LEUTNANT
LEUTNANT
Command Pistol team
Flame-thrower team
HQ SECTION
UNTEROFFIZIER
Pistol team
Pistol team
STURM SQUAD
UNTEROFFIZIER
Pistol team
Pistol team
STURM SQUAD
UNTEROFFIZIER
Pistol team
MG team
MACHINE-GUN SQUAD
UNTEROFFIZIER
Pistol team
MG team
MACHINE-GUN SQUAD
STOSS PLATOON

Stosstactik places importance on combined arms warfare. Lead units are heavily equipped with sub-machine guns and grenades to clear trenches. They are then followed-up by regular infantry with light machine-guns for mobile firepower, and flame-throwers to knock out the strongpoints. It is the start of modern infantry tactics, and will pave the way for twentieth century warfare.

WEAPONS PLATOONS

Stoss Machine-gun Platoon

Platoon

HQ Section with:

2 Maxim HMG	210 points
1 Maxim HMG	105 points

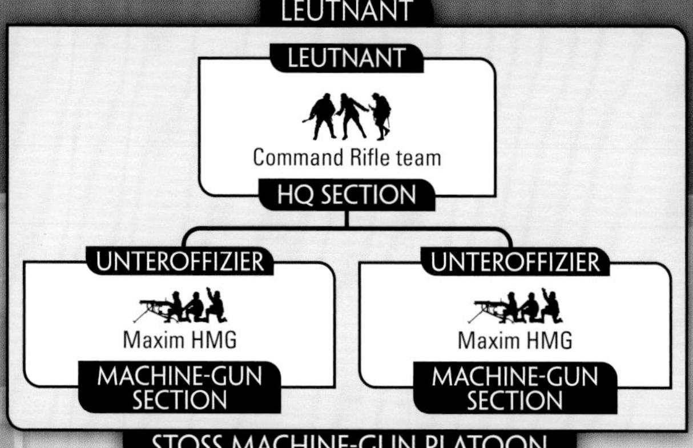

As we have seen though this war; the heavy machine gun rules no-man's land. While not as large as the HMG platoons of our regular infantry counterparts; the Maxim HMGs we have will provide us with much needed covering fire, pinning the enemy as we get into position for our assault.

Stoss Minenwerfer Platoon

Platoon

3 7.6cm Minenwerfer	570 points
2 7.6cm Minenwerfer	380 points
1 7.6cm Minenwerfer	190 points

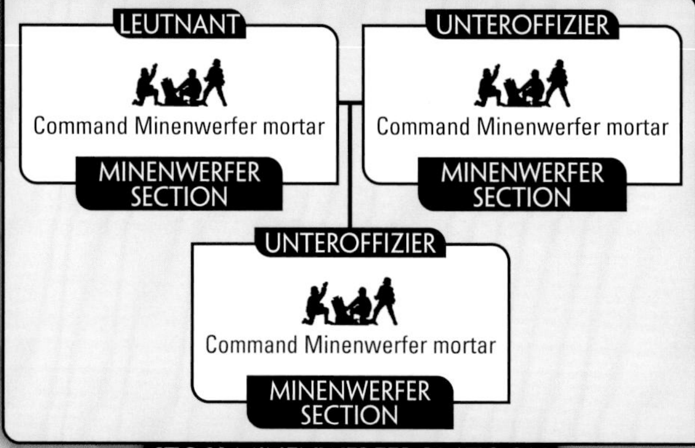

Minenwefer Sections operate as separate platoons, each gun is their own Command team.

7.6cm Minenwerfer gun teams are Trench Guns (see page 4).

While trying to avoid enemy strong points is how we fight, sometimes we cannot ignore or get around those well placed Vickers or Hotchkiss heavy machine guns of our enemy. When we encounter a weapon like that, we call on our Minenwefer's to make quick work of these troublesome weapons and then resume the advance.

German Arsenal

TANK TEAMS

Name *Weapon*	Mobility *Range*	Front *ROF*	Armour Side *Anti-tank*	Top *Firepower*	Equipment and Notes
A7V	6"/15cm	2	1	1	Four Side-mounted MG, Two hull-rear MG, Landship, Mobile fortress, Overloaded, Self-defence MG.
5.7cm Maxim-Nordenfelt gun	*24"/60cm*	*2*	*6*	*4+*	*Hull mounted.*
Beute Mark IV female	4"/10cm	1	1	1	Four Side-mounted MG, Landship, Mobile fortress Self-defence MG, Wide tracks.
Beute Mark IV male	4"/10cm	1	1	1	Landship, Self-defence MG, Wide tracks.
OQF 6 pdr gun	*24"/60cm*	*2*	*6*	*4+*	*Side mounted.*
OQF 6 pdr gun	*24"/60cm*	*2*	*6*	*4+*	*Side mounted.*

VEHICLE MACHINE-GUNS

Vehicle MG	*16"/40cm*	*3*	*3*	*6*	

INFANTRY TEAMS

Team	Range	ROF	Anti-tank	Firepower	Notes
Pistol team	4"/10cm	2	1	6	Full ROF when moving.
SMG team	4"/10cm	3	1	6	Full ROF when moving.
Rifle team	16"/40cm	1	2	6	
MG team	16"/40cm	3	2	6	ROF 2 when pinned down.
Rifle Grenade team	12"/30cm	2	1	4+	Can fire over friendly teams.
Anti-tank Rifle team	16"/40cm	1	4	5+	Tank Assault 3.
Flame-thrower team	4"/10cm	2	-	6	Flame-thrower.

ADDITIONAL TRAINING AND EQUIPMENT

Pistol and SMG teams in a Stoss Platoon are rated Tank Assault 3.

GUN TEAMS

Weapon	Mobility	Range	ROF	Anti-tank	Firepower	Notes
Maxim HMG	Man-packed	24"/60cm	6	3	6	ROF 3 when pinned down or moving.
Firing bombardments		40"/100cm	-	-	-	
Granatenwerfer mortar	Man-packed	16"/40cm	2	2	3+	Can fire over friendly teams, Minimum range 8"/20cm.
7.6cm Minenwerfer mortar	Light	32"/80cm	2	3	2+	Can fire over friendly teams, Minimum range 8"/20cm, Trench gun.
3.7cm TaK gun	Man-packed	24"/60cm	2	5	4+	No HE.
7.62cm Krupp IG gun	Light	16"/40cm	2	5	3+	Gun shield, Trench gun.
7.7cm FK96 n.A. gun	Heavy	24"/60cm	2	8	3+	Gun shield.
Firing bombardments		64"/160cm	-	3	6	

TRANSPORT TEAMS

Vehicle *Weapon*	Mobility *Range*	Front *ROF*	Armour Side *Anti-tank*	Top *Firepower*	Equipment and Notes
Horse-drawn limber	Horse-drawn	-	-	-	

FORTIFICATIONS

Weapon	Range	ROF	Anti-tank	Firepower	Notes
HMG Pillbox	24"/60cm	6	3	6	ROF 3 when pinned down.
HMG Nest	24"/60cm	6	3	6	ROF 3 when pinned down.

German tanks and infantry make their way through the town of Villers-Bretonneux.

2nd Lieutenant Frank Mitchell's Mark IV male tank knocks out the A7V 'Nixe' in history's first tank versus tank duel.

The A7V 'Nixe' takes to the field and severely damages two Mark IV female tanks from A Company.

Fast Mark A 'Whippets' charge down fleeing infantrymen as the German force begins to retreat.

Taking the Field
VILLERS-BRETONNEUX, 1918

The German March offensive had come very close to shattering the British Expeditionary Force (BEF) and breaking through to the channel. However, the exhausted German divisions had been fought to a standstill, and the drive to Amiens was halted at Villers-Bretonneux on 5 April.

After a rest period of three weeks, the Germans resumed their offensive on the morning of the 24 April 1918. The attack intended to capture the ridge west of Villers-Bretonneux, which provided a dominating position overlooking Amiens, and the strategically important rail line that ran through it.

The German attack fell on the British 8th Division, which was considered one of the best in the BEF, and one of the first selected for an increased allotment of Lewis light machine-guns. The 8th Division had suffered heavily during the March battles, losing half of its infantry strength. To make up the numbers, it was reinforced with young and inexperienced troops.

The Battle Opens

Overnight on the 24 April, the 8th Division was subjected to the heaviest barrage ever experienced by its men, according to survivors. The barrage included mustard gas and created a heavy fog. Whilst the artillery barrage fell heaviest on the rear areas, the front line was mostly subjected to fire from short range trench mortars.

The German attack was carried out by four divisions, the 77th Reserve, 228th, 243rd, and 4th Guards Infantry Divisions. These were reinforced by the first concerted use of German tanks. Thirteen of the new German A7V tanks had been bought up to the line for use in the attack, and wherever the tanks were used the line crumbled. The Germans captured about 2400 prisoners from the 8th Division and an attack supported by five tanks of these tank further south against the 58th Division yielded similar results.

The British had expected the Germans to use tanks at some point and had developed plans to try and stop a German tank attack. These included sending forward detachments of field artillery guns, either singly or in pairs, and staging tank platoons close to the front lines. The III (Third) Corps defending Villers-Bretonneux had both at hand and despatched field guns and tanks to meet the German armour.

The First Tank Battle

Captain John Brown, MC, commanded a section of three tanks from A Company, 1st Battalion, 3rd Tank Brigade and moved forward with one Mark IV male and two Mark IV female tanks. Just before being ordered to the front line, Brown's tanks were caught in a gas attack, and many of the crew were partially disabled with swollen eyes. Still, they mounted up and moved into action through the German artillery barrage.

Second Lieutenant Frank Mitchell, MC, commanded the Mark IV male tank as it trundled into combat near the small village of Cachy. After crossing through the British trenches, the riflemen inside told Mitchell that there were German tanks about. Sure enough, moments later Mitchell spotted them through his vision port and a surge of excitement bounded through the crew as they prepared for history's first tank versus tank duel.

The three British Mark IVs moved closer to a German A7V named *Nixe*. Within a few moments Mitchell saw the two females get hit by the German tank's 57mm gun. Huge holes had been ripped through the sides and rear of the machine-gun-armed tanks and they slowly limped away. The A7V pressed on, apparently not seeing Mitchell's tank approaching.

Mitchell manoeuvred his tank so that he could engage the German A7V with his 6 pounder guns. His gunner was partially blinded from the gas attack earlier and after several shots, he hit the A7V three times. Mitchell saw the German crew bail out and two other German tanks quickly withdraw. The crew celebrated their victory with loud shouts that were barely heard over the din of their machine's engines.

Mitchell's crew turned around to return to their lines, having accomplished their mission. On its way back the tank was damaged by artillery fire and the crew bailed out, returning later to reclaim their tank.

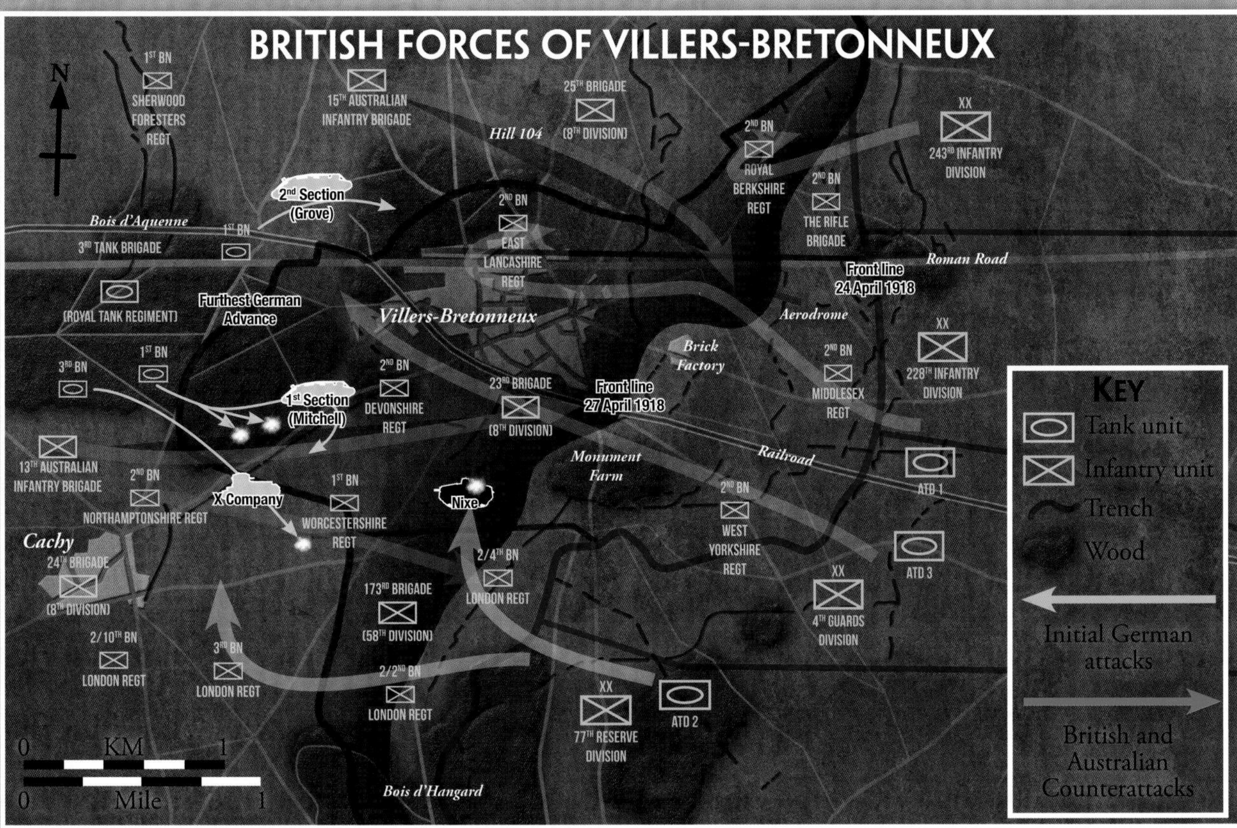

THE RIDE OF THE WHIPPETS

As Mitchell's crew returned to their tank, he saw the charge of seven Whippet medium tanks of X Company, 3rd Battalion, 3rd Tank Brigade. With the German tanks quitting the field, the attacking infantry was left on its own. The machine-gun armed Whippets used their superior speed to ride down the German infantry.

The Whippets devastated the German attack, claiming to have inflicted at least 400 casualties before the surviving troops fled. Four Whippets were knocked out in the action by a combination of fire from German artillery, trench mortars, and the A7V tanks that had returned to the front.

SHORING UP THE LINE

Another section of A Company tanks supported a successful counter attack by the 8th Division, with one male and one female Mark IV. After inflicting casualties and helping the 2nd Battalion, Royal Berkshire Regiment and the 2nd Rifle Brigade to stabilise their line, both tanks were knocked out by German field guns.

Fearing a resumption of the German offensive, the British ordered two Australian brigades to immediately counter attack and retake the village. Both of the brigade commanders refused, stating that to attack in daylight across open fields would result in excessively heavy casualties. The attack was postponed to late that night and was conducted without artillery preparatory bombardment. The German defenders were caught unawares, and the counter attack achieved complete success with relatively few casualties.

Villers-Bretonneux marked the end of the German March Offensive, as well as the final turning point of the Great War. With the successful defence of this small French town, the Allied forces gained the strategic initiative and began the offensives that would see them finally end the war.

BRITISH SPECIAL RULES

A British Rifle Company does not use any of the British special rules found in the* Flames Of War *rulebook, and instead uses the following special rules.

BRITISH BULLDOG

Some 175 years ago, a French general remarked that the British troops his infantry attacked appeared to have taken root and be stuck to the ground. They refused to run away when other troops would have. Nothing has changed and British soldiers still have a reputation for tenacity and stubbornly refusing to give up ground that they have taken.

When British platoons test their Motivation to Counterattack in assaults, you may re-roll the die and apply the re-rolled result to all British platoons that failed on the original roll.

TRENCH FIGHTERS

By 1918, the British army was the most aggressive and lethal assault force on the Western Front. Using bombers armed with hand-grenades, light-weight Lewis light-machine-guns, and fixed bayonets, British riflemen were unstoppable in hand-to-hand combat.

Rifle and Pistol teams from British Rifle Platoons (page 25) hit on a roll of 2+ in Assaults if they are Veterans (instead of 3+) or 3+ if they are Trained (instead of 4+).

Rifle Grenade and MG teams support the assault from behind the charge and therefore do not benefit from the Trench Fighters special rule.

Rifle Company

(INFANTRY COMPANY)

You must field one platoon from each box shaded black and may field one platoon from each box shaded grey.

Your Company HQ must be either from a Line Division (marked ◉), or an Elite Division (marked ✠). All other platoons with any of these symbols must be from the same division as your Company HQ.

SUPPORT PLATOONS

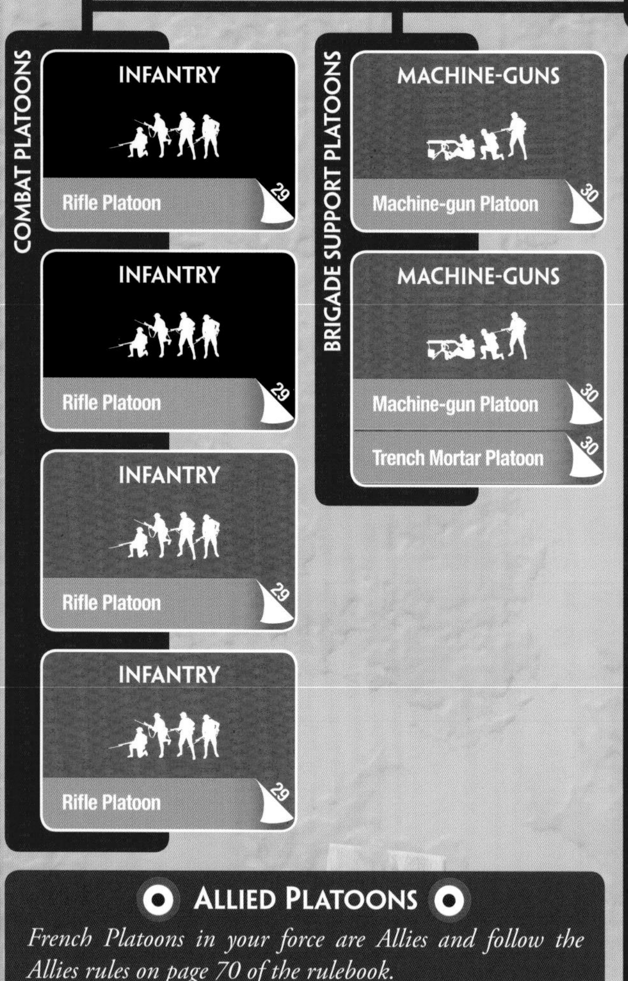

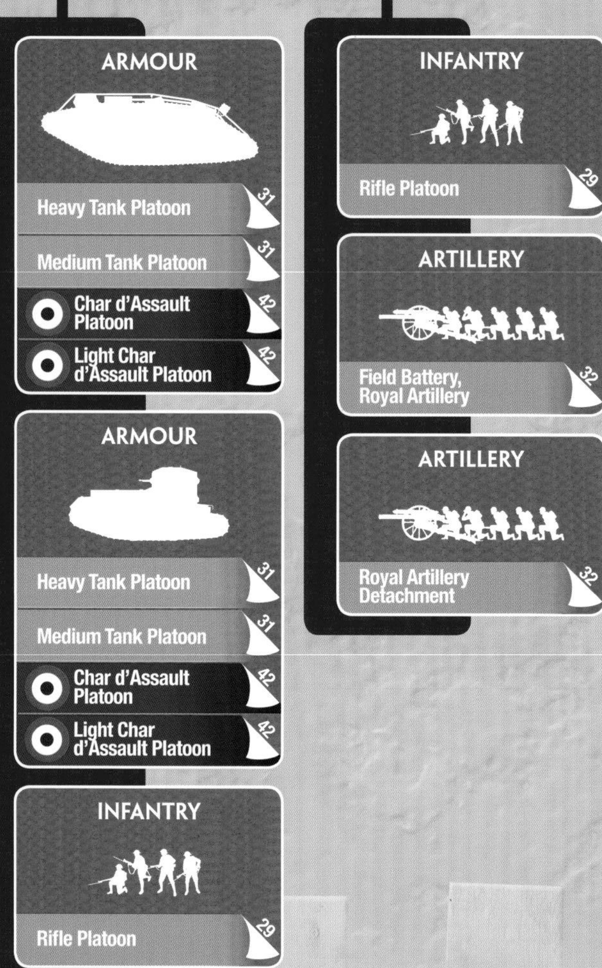

◉ ALLIED PLATOONS ◉

French Platoons in your force are Allies and follow the Allies rules on page 70 of the rulebook.

MOTIVATION AND SKILL

Two-thirds of the British divisions on the Western Front were mostly used for holding the front line. These Line Divisions are rated **Confident Trained.**

The rest were considered elite, proving themselves in offensive operations. They were usually called on when an attack was being prepared. These Elite Divisions are rated **Confident Veteran.**

LINE DIVISION	
RELUCTANT	CONSCRIPT
CONFIDENT	**TRAINED**
FEARLESS	VETERAN

ELITE DIVISION	
RELUCTANT	CONSCRIPT
CONFIDENT	TRAINED
FEARLESS	**VETERAN**

HEADQUARTERS

RIFLE COMPANY HQ

HEADQUARTERS

	Line	Elite
Company HQ	25 points	30 points

OPTION

- Add up to one Sniper team for +60 points.

After three long years of war, the British infantry are worn, but their courage has not dimmed. They can look to their officers to provide an example. The company's Major will draw his revolver and lead the men forward, as he has always done, to glorious victory.

COMBAT PLATOONS

RIFLE PLATOON

PLATOON

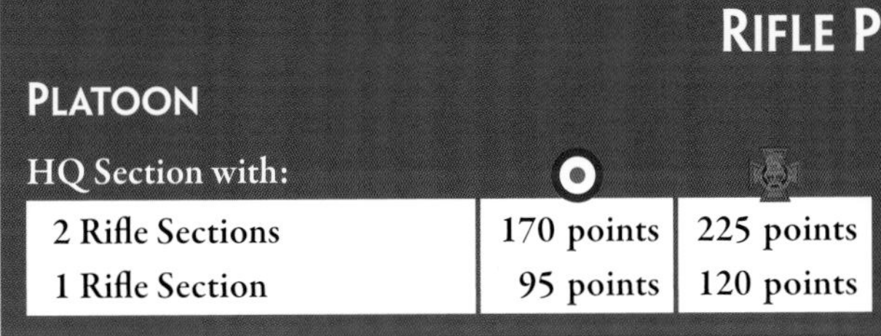

HQ Section with:

	Line	Elite
2 Rifle Sections	170 points	225 points
1 Rifle Section	95 points	120 points

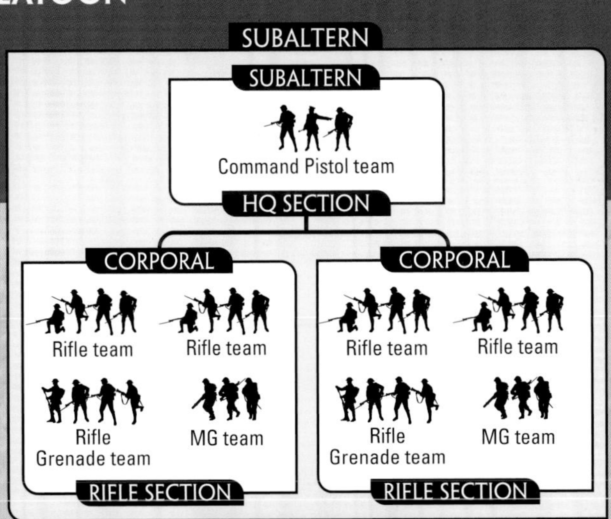

Jerry has thrown everything at us – machine gun bullets at the Somme, shells at Verdun, and their vile poison gas at Ypres – but 'Tommy' has held firm. The traditional qualities of British infantry—courage, discipline and marksmanship—have stood them in good stead along with their trusty '303' Enfield rifle.

Now, with Lewis light machine-guns, bombers, rifle grenades, and hard won experience, we are pushing the enemy back along the front. Our new recruits make up in dash what they may lack in experience. When the whistle blows, they will be ready to charge through the mud to the green fields beyond.

BRIGADE SUPPORT PLATOONS

Machine-Gun Platoon

Platoon

HQ Section with:

4 Vickers HMG	225 points	290 points
3 Vickers HMG	170 points	220 points
2 Vickers HMG	115 points	150 points

A Machine-gun Platoon may fire bombardments (see page 4).

If there is one weapon that the British infantryman trusts more than his 303, it is the Vickers machine gun. The modern Vickers is a symbol of British industry. Sturdy, with a tripod for accuracy and water-cooled for sustained fire, it is supremely reliable. The Vickers dominates the battlefield, warding off German attacks, and providing a tremendous base of fire for our men to advance under.

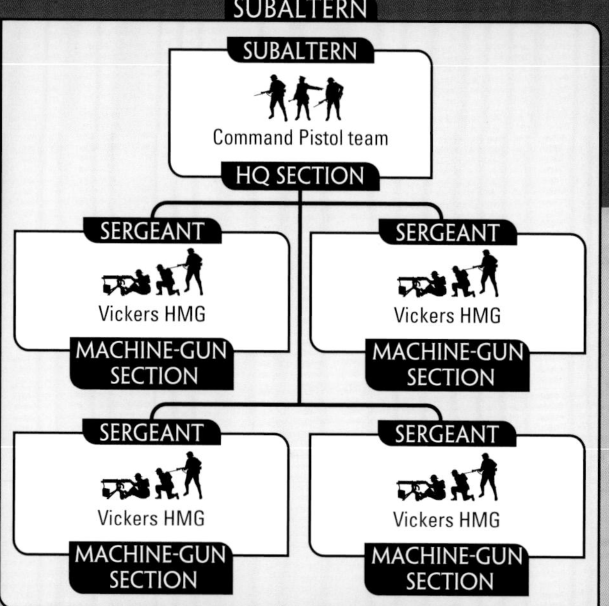

Trench Mortar Platoon

Platoon

4 3" Stokes	280 points	360 points
3 3" Stokes	210 points	270 points
2 3" Stokes	140 points	180 points
1 3" Stokes	70 points	90 points

Mortar Sections operate as separate platoons, each gun is their own Command team.

3" Stokes mortar teams are Trench Guns (see page 4).

Trench warfare has highlighted the need for the forward infantry to have heavy fire support with them to knock out enemy defences. The new Stokes mortar has been designed to do the job, and is just the ticket. It has good range, rate of fire, and firepower, thanks to its three-inch shell.

SUBALTERN

SUBALTERN — Command 3" Stokes mortar — MORTAR SECTION

SERGEANT — Command 3" Stokes mortar — MORTAR SECTION

SUBALTERN — Command 3" Stokes mortar — MORTAR SECTION

SERGEANT — Command 3" Stokes mortar — MORTAR SECTION

TRENCH MORTAR PLATOON

SUPPORT PLATOONS

HEAVY TANK PLATOON

PLATOON

	Points	Points (Veteran)
4 Mark IV female	800 points	1040 points
3 Mark IV female	600 points	780 points
2 Mark IV female	400 points	520 points
1 Mark IV female	200 points	260 points

Replace any or all Mark IV female tanks with:

Mark IV male	+60 points	+80 points

4 Mark V female	-	1160 points
3 Mark V female	-	870 points
2 Mark V female	-	580 points
1 Mark V female	-	290 points

Replace any or all Mark V female tanks with:

Mark V male	-	+85 points
Mark V hermaphrodite	-	+65 points
Mark V* female	-	no cost
Mark V* male	-	+85 points
Mark V* hermaphrodite	-	+65 points

CAPTAIN

CAPTAIN — Command tank — TANK SECTION

SUBALTERN — Command tank — TANK SECTION

SUBALTERN — Command tank — TANK SECTION

SUBALTERN — Command tank — TANK SECTION

HEAVY TANK PLATOON

Tank Sections operate as separate platoons, each tank is their own Command team.

A Rifle Company that includes a Heavy Tank Platoon will Always Attack, unless it also includes an Field Battery, Royal Artillery, which will make it Always Defend.

The British Army has applied its technological superiority to develop a new weapon—the tank—to achieve decisive breakthroughs on the battlefield. A year on since their debut at Messines Ridge, the Mark IV version is now in full production, with improved armour and fire protection. The tanks are armed as either male (with two six-pounder guns) or female (with four machine guns) versions.

Also arriving at the front are the new Mark V tanks with improved reliability and new variants like the Mark V* with it lengthened body to carry of section of troops.

MEDIUM TANK PLATOON

PLATOON

	Points	Points (Veteran)
5 Mark A Whippet	650 points	850 points
4 Mark A Whippet	520 points	680 points
3 Mark A Whippet	390 points	510 points
2 Mark A Whippet	260 points	340 points
1 Mark A Whippet	130 points	170 points

CAPTAIN

CAPTAIN — Command Mark A Whippet — HQ TANK

SUBALTERN — Command Mark A Whippet — TANK SECTION

SUBALTERN — Command Mark A Whippet — TANK SECTION

SUBALTERN — Command Mark A Whippet — TANK SECTION

SUBALTERN — Command Mark A Whippet — TANK SECTION

MEDIUM TANK PLATOON

Tank Sections operate as separate platoons, each tank is their own Command team.

A Rifle Company that includes a Medium Tank Platoon will Always Attack, unless it also includes an Field Battery, Royal Artillery, which will make it Always Defend.

The latest development from British industry, the Whippet medium tank, is designed to follow up and exploit the breakthroughs that are made by the heavy tanks. The 8-mile-per-hour speed of the Whippet will enable it to surge ahead and complements the strength and firepower of the Mark IV and V.

Field Battery, Royal Artillery

Platoon

HQ Section with:	◉	VC
6 OQF 18 pdr	810 points	1055 points
3 OQF 18 pdr	425 points	555 points

Option

- Add horse-drawn limbers for +5 points for the battery.

A Rifle Company that includes a Field Battery, Royal Artillery will Always Defend.

The Ordnance Quick Firing 18 pounder (84mm) gun is our standard field piece and the backbone of the Royal Artillery. It fires a heavier shell than the French 75mm or German 77mm, and is accurate, reliable, and has good range. Combined with the well-trained crews of the Royal Artillery, the 18 pounder can out-shoot any foe.

CAPTAIN

CAPTAIN

Command Pistol team

HQ TROOP

LIEUTENANT

OQF 18 pdr gun

Horse-drawn limber

OQF 18 pdr gun

Horse-drawn limber

OQF 18 pdr gun

Horse-drawn limber

GUN SECTION

LIEUTENANT

OQF 18 pdr gun

Horse-drawn limber

OQF 18 pdr gun

Horse-drawn limber

OQF 18 pdr gun

Horse-drawn limber

GUN SECTION

FIELD BATTERY, ROYAL ARTILLERY

Royal Artillery Detachment

Platoon

	◉	VC
2 OQF 18 pdr	260 points	340 points
1 OQF 18 pdr	130 points	170 points

Option

- Add horse-drawn limbers for +5 points for the platoon.

Gun Sections operate as separate platoons, each gun is their own Command team.

LIEUTENANT

LIEUTENANT

Command OQF 18 pdr gun

Horse-drawn limber

GUN SECTION

SERGEANT

Command OQF 18 pdr gun

Horse-drawn limber

GUN SECTION

ROYAL ARTILLERY DETACHMENT

The OQF 18 pounder field gun is mobile for its size, which lends it to use by forward detachments. The Royal Artillery are learning to operate in small units attached to the front line infantry to help deal with German tanks or offer direct fire to knock out enemy gun emplacements.

British Arsenal

TANK TEAMS

Name *Weapon*	Mobility *Range*	Front *ROF*	Armour Side *Anti-tank*	Top *Firepower*	Equipment and Notes
HEAVY TANKS					
Mark IV female	4"/10cm	1	1	1	Four Side-mounted MG, Landship, Mobile fortress, Self-defence MG, Wide tracks.
Mark IV male	4"/10cm	1	1	1	Landship, Self-defence MG, Wide tracks.
OQF 6 pdr gun	*24"/60cm*	*2*	*6*	*4+*	*Side mounted.*
OQF 6 pdr gun	*24"/60cm*	*2*	*6*	*4+*	*Side mounted.*
Mark V female	4"/10cm	1	1	1	Four Side-mounted MG, Landship, Mobile fortress, Self-defence MG, Reliable, Wide tracks.
Mark V male	4"/10cm	1	1	1	Landship, Self-defence MG, Reliable, Wide tracks.
OQF 6 pdr gun	*24"/60cm*	*2*	*6*	*4+*	*Side mounted.*
OQF 6 pdr gun	*24"/60cm*	*2*	*6*	*4+*	*Side mounted.*
Mark V hermaphrodite	4"/10cm	1	1	1	Two Side-mounted MG, Landship, Self-defence MG, Reliable, Wide tracks.
OQF 6 pdr gun	*24"/60cm*	*2*	*6*	*4+*	*Side mounted.*
Mark V* female	4"/10cm	1	1	1	Carries three passengers, Four Side-mounted MG, Landship, Mobile fortress, Rough ride, Self-defence MG, Very wide tracks.
Mark V* male	4"/10cm	1	1	1	Carries three passengers, Landship, Rough ride, Self-defence MG, Very wide tracks.
OQF 6 pdr gun	*24"/60cm*	*2*	*6*	*4+*	*Side mounted.*
OQF 6 pdr gun	*24"/60cm*	*2*	*6*	*4+*	*Side mounted.*
Mark V* hermaphrodite	4"/10cm	1	1	1	Carries three passengers, Two Side-mounted MG Landship, Self-defence MG, Rough ride, Very wide tracks.
OQF 6 pdr gun	*24"/60cm*	*2*	*6*	*4+*	*Side mounted.*
MEDIUM TANK					
Mark A Whippet	8"/20cm	1	1	1	Two MG.
VEHICLE MACHINE-GUNS					
Vehicle MG	*16"/40cm*	*3*	*2*	*6*	

INFANTRY TEAMS

Team	Range	ROF	Anti-tank	Firepower	Notes
Pistol team	4"/10cm	2	1	6	Full ROF when moving.
Rifle team	16"/40cm	1	2	6	
MG team	16"/40cm	3	2	6	ROF 2 when pinned down.
Rifle Grenade team	12"/30cm	2	1	4+	Can fire over friendly teams.

GUN TEAMS

Weapon	Mobility	Range	ROF	Anti-tank	Firepower	Notes
Vickers HMG	Man-packed	24"/60cm	6	2	6	ROF 3 when pinned down or moving.
Firing bombardments		40"/100cm	-	-	-	
3" Stokes mortar	Light	24"/60cm	2	2	3+	Can fire over friendly teams, Minimum range 8"/20cm, Trench gun.
OQF 18 pdr gun	Heavy	24"/60cm	2	8	3+	Gun shield.
Firing bombardments		64"/160cm	-	3	5+	

TRANSPORT TEAMS

Vehicle *Weapon*	Mobility *Range*	Front *ROF*	Side *Anti-tank*	Armour Top *Firepower*	Equipment and Notes
Horse-drawn limber	Horse-drawn	-	-	-	

FORTIFICATIONS

Weapon	Range	ROF	Anti-tank	Firepower	Notes
HMG Pillbox	24"/60cm	6	2	6	ROF 3 when pinned down.
HMG Nest	24"/60cm	6	2	6	ROF 3 when pinned down.

BRITISH DECALS

The decal sheet included in the Mark IV (GBBX01), Mark V (GBBX02), and Mark V* (GBBX03) boxes allows you to field up to five differently marked British heavy tanks as found on the sheet. With a little more creative cutting you can field a much wider variety of tank markings. The diagram below shows where numbers and names are usually placed.

The decal sheet also includes German crosses for fielding *Beute Mk IV* (Captured Mark IV) tanks as seen in the photograph on the bottom right.

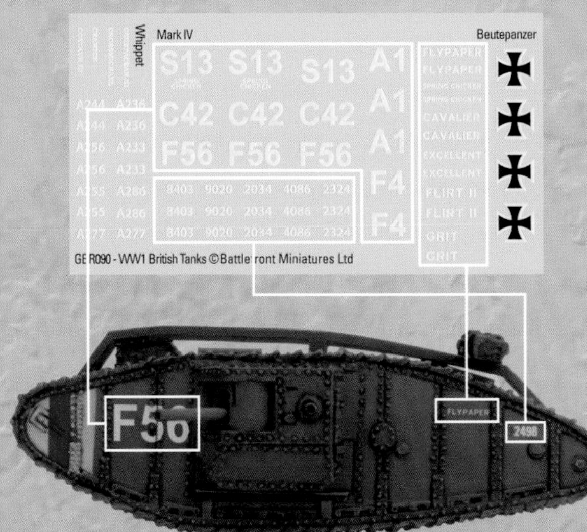

French Tanks to the Front

Battle of Soissons, 18 to 19 July 1918

No country is a better example of the cataclysm of the Great War than France. In 1914 France quickly joined the conflict to live up to its commitment to Russia. As soon as France declared war on Germany, they then executed Plan XVII, an attack on the borders of Germany to regain the territories lost in the Franco-Prussian War. Germany and France were historical enemies and the troops of 1914 marched off to a cheering public, in uniforms and tactics reminiscent of the previous century. The French attack into Germany was defeated, and Germany successfully counterattacked. France suffered greatly and would have lost Paris itself if not for the 'Miracle of the Marne.' Over the next few years France suffered a bloodletting at Verdun, endured mutiny, and by 1918 was a shell of a force that marched off in 1914.

By 1918, the brilliant uniforms of 1914 were gone as were many of the men who first went to war. The *Poilu* (slang for a French Soldier) of 1918 was weary of battle, however they knew that they had to fight on to remove the hated Germans from French soil. The *Poilu* lost faith in the leaders who committed them in frontal assaults with little strategic purpose and in the late war lost much of the desire they had to attack as compared to the start of the war.

Despite the disturbing conditions the *Poilu* found themselves in during 1918, two events caused them to retain hope and carry on with the fight to defeat Germany. The first event was the United States entry into the war, arriving in French ports at a pace of 10,000 troops a week. The Americans represented fresh manpower so desperately needed. Another event which rallied the French was the German offensives of 1918, brought about by the Germans trying to win the war before the Americans could become involved. The German offensive only served to unite the Allies under a single commander, and strengthen their will to fight.

Battle of Soissons

In May and June of 1918 the fourth German offensive was stopped in its tracks as it threatened Paris, in what is known as the Second Battle of the Marne. The Allies, united under the command of Ferdinand Foch, saw that the Germans were spent and planned a counterattack. In what became the Battle of Soissons, 24 French divisions, supported by the British, Americans, and even Italians attacked the exhausted Germans and recaptured most of the ground they gained in their latest push on Paris.

The battle of Soissons was to be a turning point in 1918 and a reinvigoration of the French offensive spirit and saw the first mass use of French tanks in the war. While the British and even the Germans fielded tanks on the battlefield the French did not sit idle and also started designing and fielding tanks. The attack on Soissons featured 350 French tanks, and included the debut of the Renault FT-17. This new French tank was a departure from the previous tanks used in battle; they were smaller and had a crew of two men. The FT-17 also featured a rotating turret, which would become a mainstay on tanks today. Impressed with the FT-17, they were used by the Americans as well as many other nations. The FT-17 remained in service many decades later, when it saw action again on French soil in 1940.

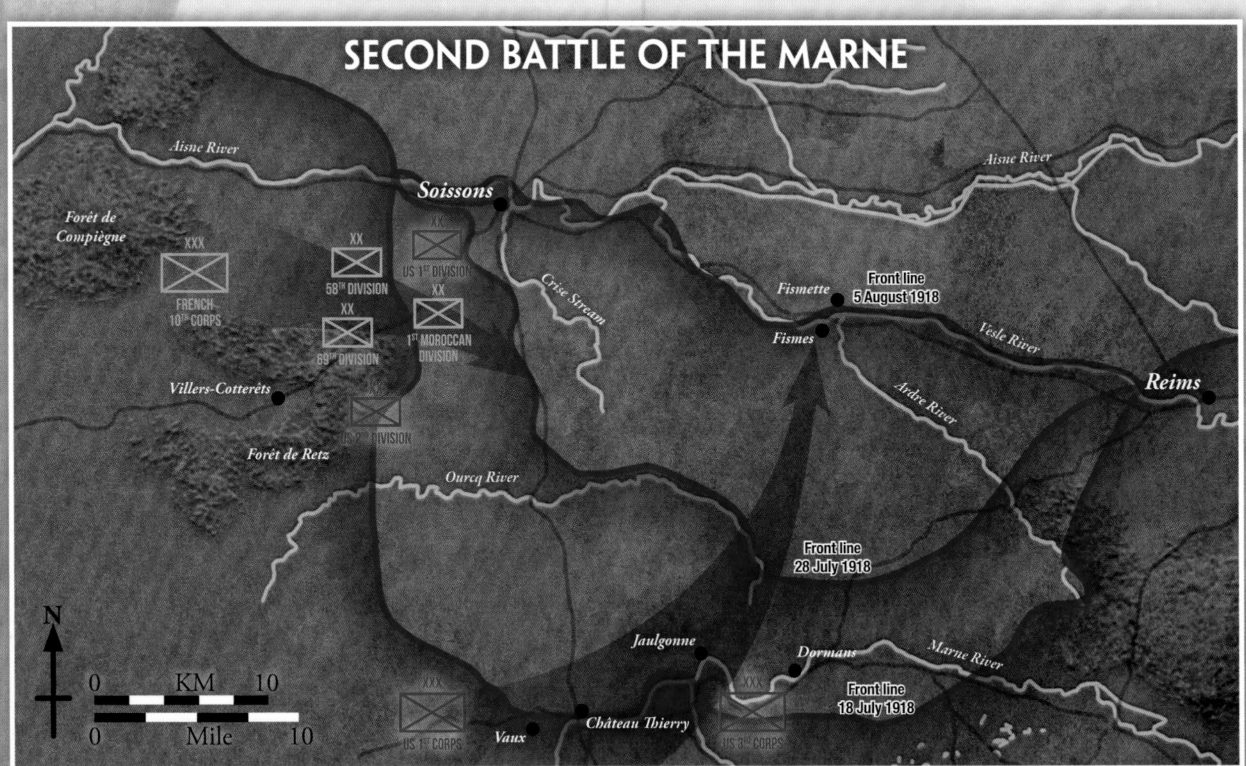

Colonial and Metropolitan Troops

At the start of the war the French Army was a huge organization with a large standing army and three classes of reservists that could be called back to the colours. This large manpower pool became necessary as the fighting of 1914-1917 took its toll, which caused the French to draft men up to the age of 45 and look to its colonies for help. While the French army was organized much like the other armies of Europe, it had some distinct differences such as the makeup of the men who filled the ranks of the French army.

At the start of the war, most of the active units and mobilized reservists were from Metropolitan France, which is limited to mainland France and the islands nearby such as Corsica. France like many other European nations had mandatory conscription, in which each year 21 year old men would be called to serve for a period of three years. Once finished with their active service commitment, the draftees would stay in the Reserve or Territorial Army until the age of 48.

The Great War represented more than nations fighting against each other, but rather empires at war. This is especially evident with the British and French, who could call upon troops from its far flung empire to serve under the colours. In 1914, the French empire included North Africa, Sub-Saharan Africa, and Indo-China. Known by the French as *'tirailleur'* (which means skirmisher or light infantry) units, these forces were recruited from places such as Senegal, Morocco, Algeria, Tunisia, and what is today Vietnam and Cambodia. The French were lucky that many of these regions produced troops that had a warrior spirit, and were fierce fighters when engaged in battle. The regional recruiting of these units ensured that they would maintain a high morale since they were fighting alongside people from the same village or tribe. Despite not being used to the harsh climates of Europe, these units fought bravely and were feared by their enemy.

Alongside the *tirailleur* units, France also had colonial troops made up of native Frenchmen. These troops were made up of either Frenchmen who settled within the French empire or from French units that served overseas protecting the French empire. After 1915, many of these types of colonial battalions were grouped with *tirailleur* units and formed *'regiments de marche'*. Giving the French much needed manpower when they needed it most, these troops from around the world played a major role in the defeat of the German army.

One aspect that was unique with the French army is that its officers could and often did serve in both metropolitan and colonial units. This rotation of officers lead to the familiarity and cohesion of these two distinct manpower pools, which helped them work together throughout the Great War.

The *Poilu* of 1918 was tired and weary of war, but in their hearts they knew that they had to carry the fight to the Germans and expel them from their homeland.

French Special Rules

A French Companie de Fusiliers uses the following national special rules.

They Shall Not Pass

Despite a number of mutinies during 1917, the French were still stubborn fighters in 1918, often unwilling to give up positions easily during the German spring offensives. They held tough, and did not needlessly give ground.

When French platoons test their Motivation to Counterattack in assaults, you may re-roll the die and apply the re-rolled result to all French platoons that failed on the original roll.

Quick Fire

The *canon de 75mm mle 1897* is a superb piece of French engineering. It was the first gun in the world to combine a breech-loading weapon with an effective recoil system. This quick-firing weapon made every other artillery piece obsolete.

Re-roll all failed To Hit rolls from Artillery Bombardments with at least four 75mm mle 1897 guns in total. Batteries with one to three 75mm mle 1897 guns do not need to re-roll successful To Hit rolls.

Trench Fighters

The French had adopted well drilled grenade tactics by 1918, using them aggressively in both attack and defence. Using grenadiers with hand-grenades, light-weight Chauchat light-machine-guns, VB rifle-grenadiers, fixed bayonets, and their natural *élan,* trenches were taken with an aggressive spirit.

Rifle and Pistol teams from French Fusiliers Platoons (page 40) hit on a roll of 2+ in Assaults (instead of 3+ for being veterans).

VB and MG teams support the assault from behind the charge and therefore do not benefit from the Trench Fighters special rule.

Trench Warfare

French troops are trained for trench warfare. Their operational plan is to make a short deliberate advance under cover of massed artillery fire, then fortify their position to hold it while the artillery comes up to repeat the process. While the advance is slow, it is sure and will eventually result in the defeat of the enemy.

When conducting Defensive Fire, Infantry and Gun teams that are Dug In or in Entrenchments can shoot over any Man-packed or Light Gun teams that are also Dug In or in Entrenchments.

COMPANIE DE FUSILIERS

(RIFLE COMPANY)

INFANTRY COMPANY

You must field one platoon from each box shaded black and may field one platoon from each box shaded grey.

Your Company HQ must be either Metropolitan (marked) or Colonial (marked). All Platoons with these symbols must be the same type as your Company HQ.

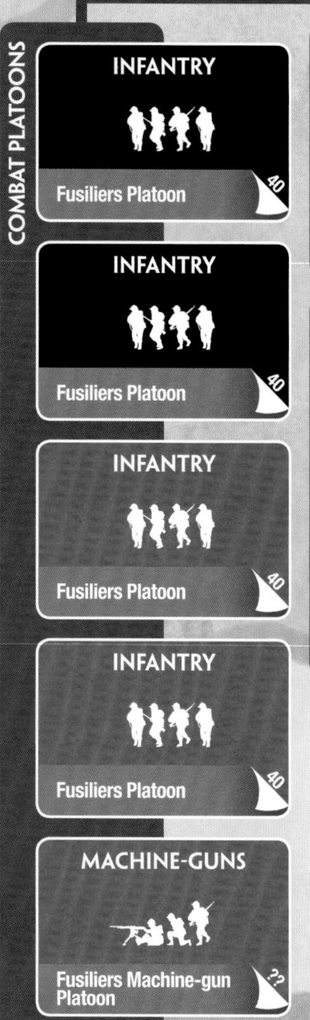

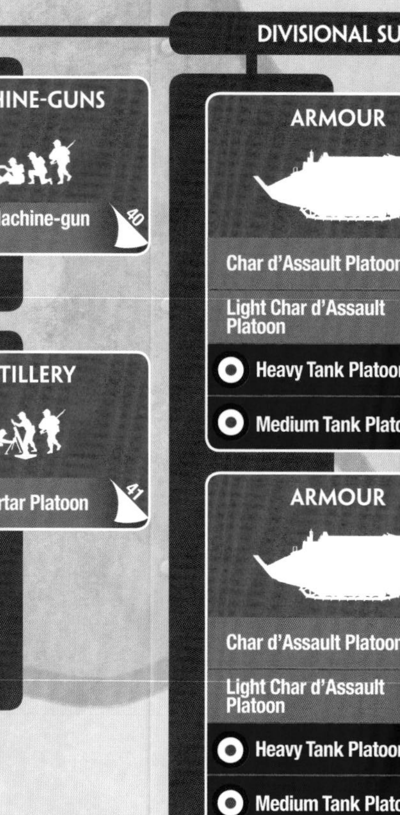

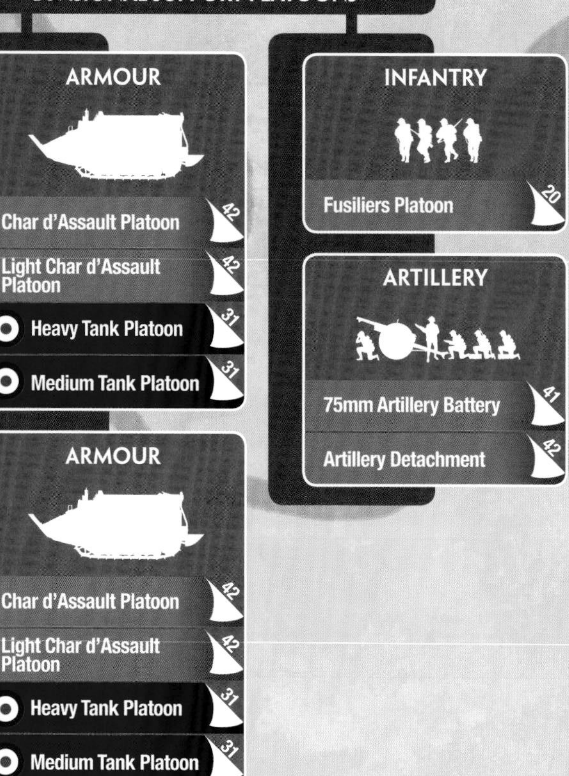

ALLIED PLATOONS

British Platoons in your force are Allies and follow the Allies rules on page 70 of the rulebook.

Motivation and Skill

A Metropolitan Companie de Fusiliers is rated as **Reluctant Veteran**.

A Colonial Companie de Fusiliers is rated as **Fearless Veteran**.

Metropolitan	
RELUCTANT	CONSCRIPT
CONFIDENT	TRAINED
FEARLESS	**VETERAN**

Colonial	
RELUCTANT	CONSCRIPT
CONFIDENT	TRAINED
FEARLESS	**VETERAN**

HEADQUARTERS

Companie de Fusiliers HQ

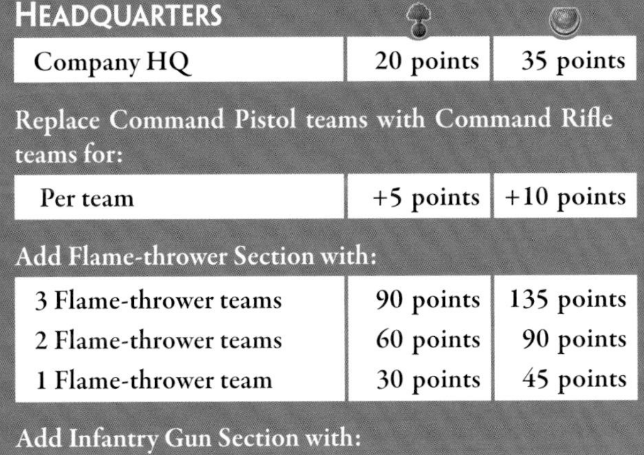

Headquarters

	Metropolitan	Colonial
Company HQ	20 points	35 points

Replace Command Pistol teams with Command Rifle teams for:

Per team	+5 points	+10 points

Add Flame-thrower Section with:

3 Flame-thrower teams	90 points	135 points
2 Flame-thrower teams	60 points	90 points
1 Flame-thrower team	30 points	45 points

Add Infantry Gun Section with:

2 37mm mle 1916	90 points	130 points
1 37mm mle 1916	45 points	65 points

Option

- Add up to one Sniper team for +60 points.

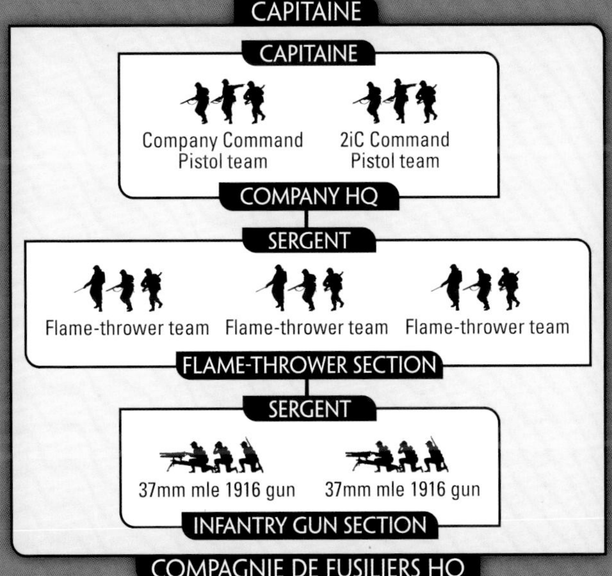

Here in 1918 our company has changed from its early war composition and is well adapted to handle the rigours of trench warfare. Artillery, trench mortars and guns, and even tanks have been incorporated into the unit in order to go on the offensive and push the Boche out of our homeland.

Knowing that the war is nearly over some of our older *Poilu* may be cautious and a bit weary of the fight; however the spirit of our colonial troops is excellent and they are ready to resume the offensive.

COMBAT PLATOONS

FUSILIERS PLATOON

PLATOON

2 Fusiliers Half-Platoons each with:

2 Fusiliers Squads	320 points	500 points

1 Fusiliers Half-Platoon with:

2 Fusiliers Squads	160 points	250 points

Fusiliers Half-Platoons operate as separate platoons, each with their own command team.

The sharp end of our fighting force is the rifleman, much the same as it was in the days of Napoleon. Supported by Chauchat light machine guns and Vivien and Bessières rifles our Fusiliers can handle any challenge in the attack or on defence. When we close in on the enemy our preferred weapon is the bayonet and the *Boche* can see how much we have learned since 1914!

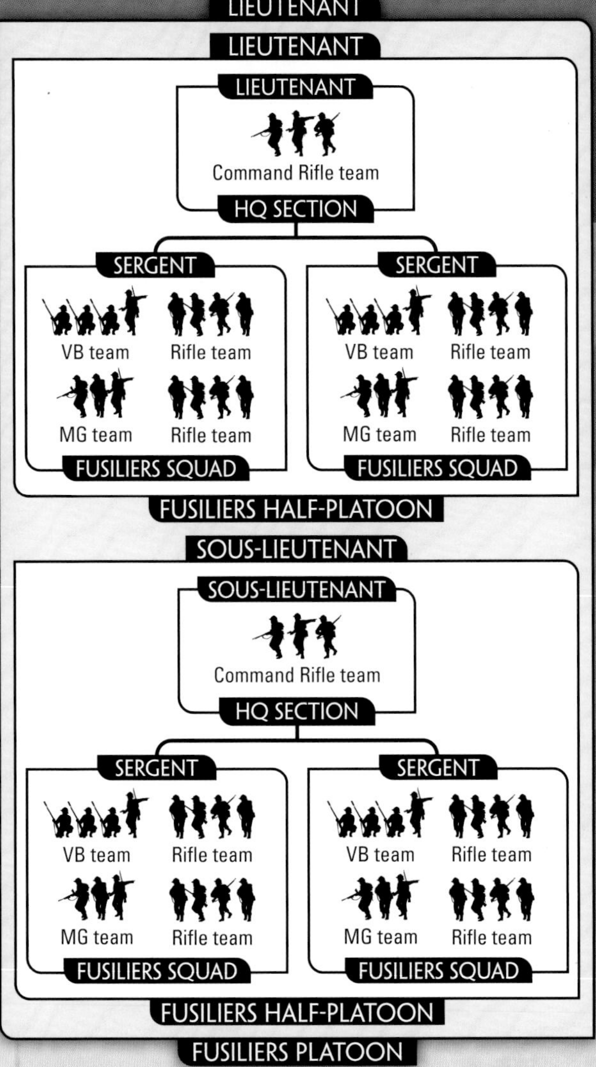

FUSILIERS MACHINE-GUN PLATOON

PLATOON

HQ Section with:

4 Hotchkiss mle 1914 HMG	225 points	330 points
3 Hotchkiss mle 1914 HMG	170 points	250 points
2 Hotchkiss mle 1914 HMG	115 points	170 points

In addition, a Fusiliers Machine-gun Platoon may fire bombardments (see page 4).

In the front lines our company is supported by the new Hochkiss mle 1914 heavy machine gun. It fires the same cartridge as our standard rifles and can sustain a rate of fire of 450 rounds per minute. Well placed in defence these guns will make the Germans think twice about attacking our front line.

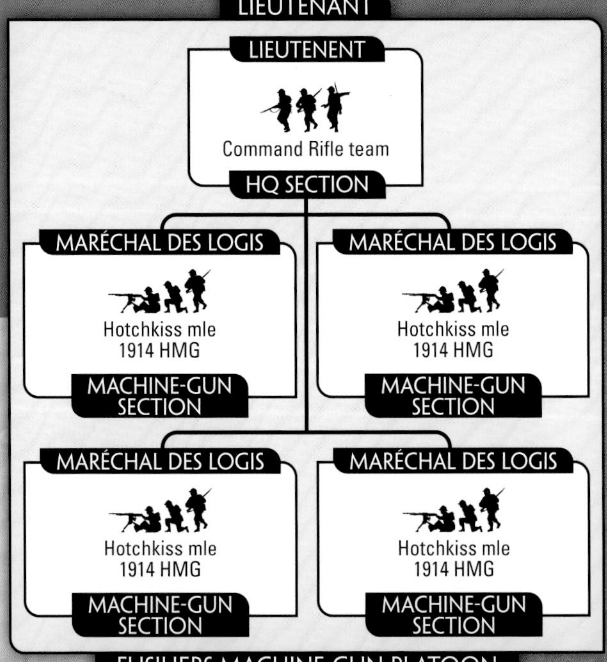

REGIMENTAL SUPPORT PLATOONS

Trench Mortar Platoon

Platoon

4 76mm Stokes	280 points	420 points
3 76mm Stokes	210 points	315 points
2 76mm Stokes	140 points	210 points
1 76mm Stokes	70 points	105 points
4 58mm Type 2	360 points	460 points
3 58mm Type 2	270 points	345 points
2 58mm Type 2	180 points	230 points
1 58mm Type 2	90 points	115 points

Mortar Sections operate as separate platoons, each gun is their own Command team.

76mm Stokes and 58mm Type 2 mortar teams are Trench Guns (see page 4).

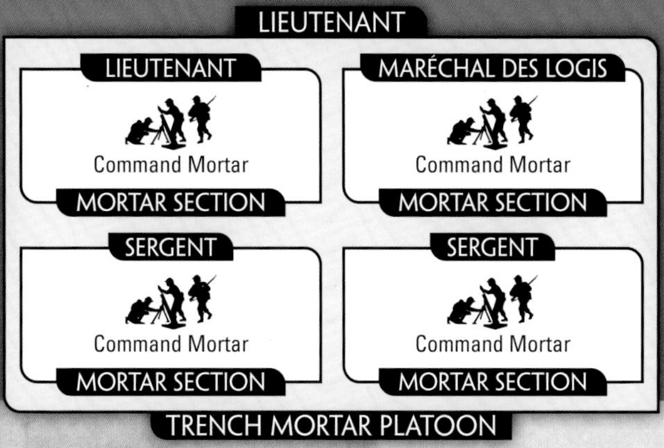

German machine gun nests and pillboxes are not the obstacle they once were due to our excellent collection of trench mortars. The British 76mm Stokes mortar can knock out strong points up close in the attack. The heavier 58mm Type 2 mortars will stay in our trench line or close behind it to knock out the most difficult of enemy positions.

DIVISIONAL SUPPORT PLATOONS

75mm Artillery Battery

Platoon

HQ Section with:

4 75mm mle 1897	545 points
2 75mm mle 1897	275 points

Option

- Add horse-drawn limbers for +5 points for the battery.

A Companie de Fusiliers that includes a 75mm Artillery Battery will Always Defend.

A 75mm Artillery Battery is rated: **Reluctant Veteran.** RELUCTANT | VETERAN

Entering into this war our 75mm mle 1897 was the world's best artillery piece; and four years of war has only improved its reputation. This gun, known for its quick fire, can bombard German positions anywhere on the front and can pin down the *Boche* until we close in.

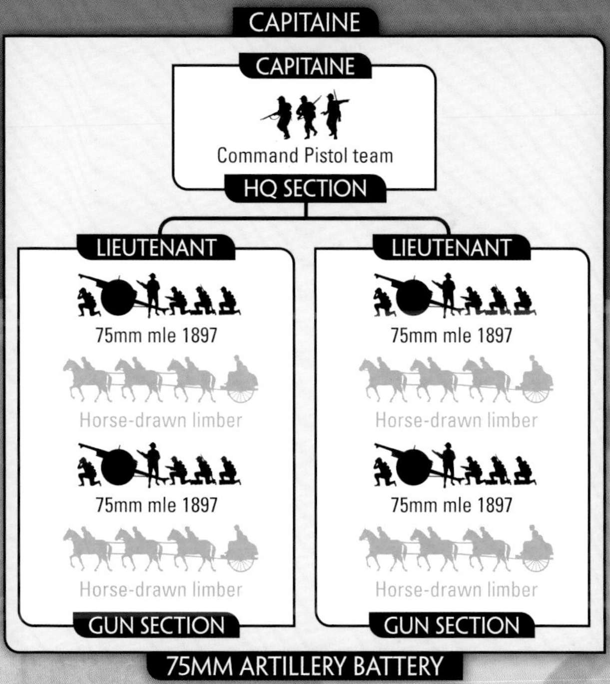

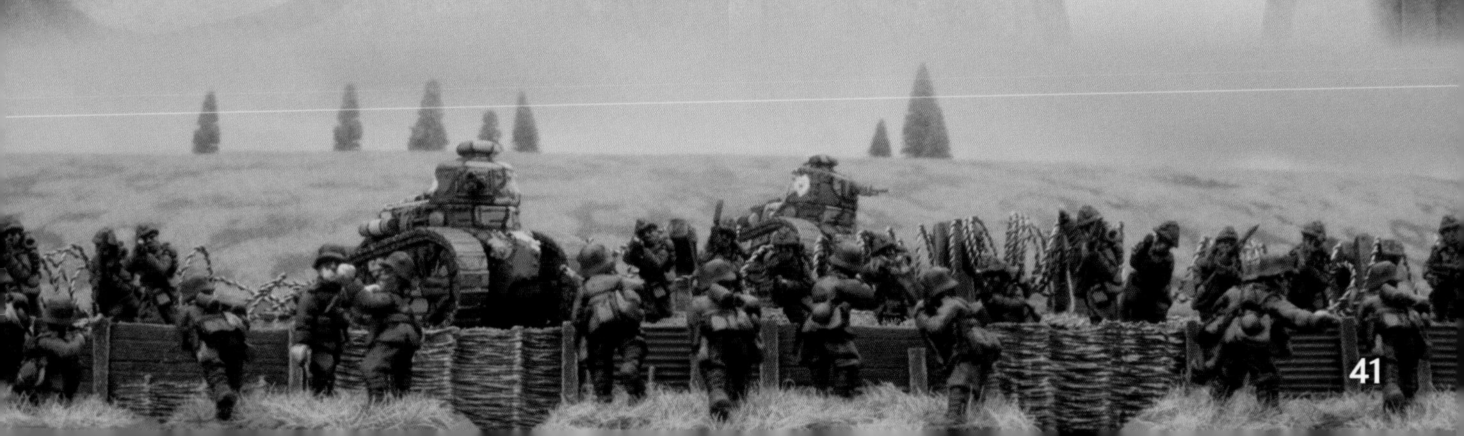

ARTILLERY DETACHMENT

PLATOON

2 75mm mle 1897	260 points
1 75mm mle 1897	130 points

OPTION

- Add horse-drawn limbers for +5 points for the platoon.

An Artillery Detachment is rated **Reluctant Veteran.**

RELUCTANT | VETERAN

LIEUTENANT

ARTILLERY DETACHMENT

Each Gun Section operates as separate platoons, each gun is their own Command team.

CHAR D'ASSAULT PLATOON

PLATOON

4 Schneider CA.1	800 points
3 Schneider CA.1	600 points
2 Schneider CA.1	400 points
1 Schneider CA.1	200 points
4 Char Saint Chamond	1260 points
3 Char Saint Chamond	945 points
2 Char Saint Chamond	630 points
1 Char Saint Chamond	315 points

Each Tank in a Char d'Assault Platoon operates as separate platoon, each tanks is their own Command team.

A Char d'Assault Platoon is rated **Confident Trained.**

CONFIDENT | TRAINED

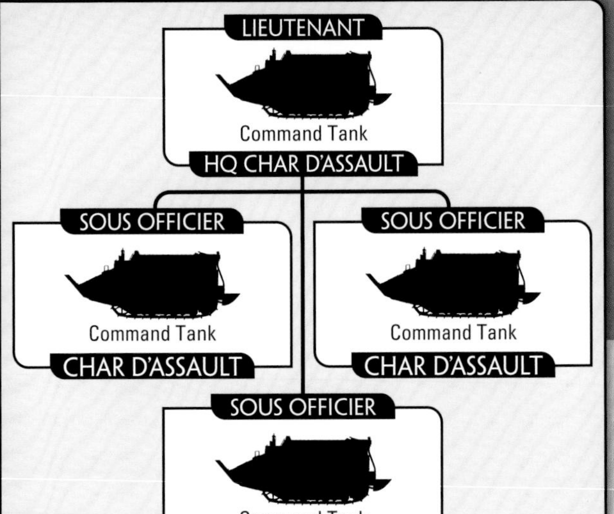

Our heavy tanks feature the first French tank, the Schneider CA1. While it had its drawbacks, it supported us well in the past. Now joined with the Saint-Chamond, which features our excellent 75mm gun, we have a collection of heavy tanks that can dominate no-mans land and support our *Poilu* in the attack.

LIGHT CHAR D'ASSAULT PLATOON

PLATOON

3 Renault FT-17 (37mm) and 2 Renault FT-17 (MG)	565 points
2 Renault FT-17 (37mm) and 2 Renault FT-17 (MG)	440 points
2 Renault FT-17 (37mm) and 1 Renault FT-17 (MG)	345 points
1 Renault FT-17 (37mm) and 1 Renault FT-17 (MG)	220 points

A Light Char d'Assault Platoon is rated **Confident Trained.**

CONFIDENT | TRAINED

LIEUTENANT

LIEUTENANT
Command Renault FT-17 (37mm)
HQ SECTION

SOUS OFFICIER
Renault FT-17 (37mm) | Renault FT-17 (MG)
CHAR D'ASSAULT SECTION

CAPORAL
Renault FT-17 (37mm) | Renault FT-17 (MG)
CHAR D'ASSAULT SECTION

LIGHT CHAR D'ASSAULT PLATOON

French Arsenal

Tank Teams

Name *Weapon*	Mobility *Range*	Armour Front *ROF*	 Side *Anti-tank*	 Top *Firepower*	Equipment and Notes
TANKS					
Renault FT-17 (MG)	6"/15cm	1	1	1	Overloaded, Turret MG.
Renault FT-17 (37mm) *37mm SA-18 gun*	6"/15cm *16"/40cm*	1 *2*	1 *4*	1 *4+*	Overloaded. *One-man turret.*
Schneider CA.1 *75mm Blockhaus Schneider*	4"/10cm *16"/40cm*	1 *2*	1 *5*	1 *3+*	Two side-mounted MG, Landship, Overloaded. *Side mounted.*
Char Saint Chamond *75mm mle 1897 gun*	4"/10cm *24"/60cm*	1 *2*	1 *8*	1 *3+*	Hull MG, Two side-mounted MG, Hull-rear MG, Landship, Overloaded. *Hull mounted.*

Gun Teams

Weapon	Mobility	Range	ROF	Anti-tank	Firepower	Notes
Hotchkiss mle 1914 HMG Firing bombardments	Man-packed	24"/60cm 40"/100cm	6 -	2 -	6 -	ROF 3 when pinned down or moving.
76mm Stokes mortar	Light	24"/60cm	2	2	3+	Can fire over friendly teams, Minimum range 8"/20cm, Trench gun.
58mm Type 2 mortar	Medium	32"/80cm	2	2	2+	Can fire over friendly teams, Minimum range 8"/20cm, Trench gun.
37mm mle 1916 gun	Man-packed	16"/40cm	3	4	4+	
75mm mle 1897 gun Firing bombardments	Heavy	24"/60cm 64"/160cm	2 -	8 3	3+ 6	Gun shield, Quick fire.

Infantry Teams

Team	Range	ROF	Anti-tank	Firepower	Notes
Pistol team	4"/10cm	2	1	6	Full ROF when moving, Trench fighters.
Rifle team	16"/40cm	1	2	6	Trench fighters.
MG team	16"/40cm	3	2	6	ROF 2 when pinned down.
VB team	8"/20cm	2	1	4+	Can fire over friendly teams.
Flame-thrower team	4"/10cm	2	-	6	Flame-thrower.

Transport Teams

Vehicle *Weapon*	Mobility *Range*	Front *ROF*	Side *Anti-tank*	Armour Top *Firepower*	Equipment and Notes
Horse-drawn limber	Horse-drawn	-	-	-	

Fortifications

Weapon	Range	ROF	Anti-tank	Firepower	Notes
HMG Pillbox	24"/60cm	6	2	6	ROF 3 when pinned down.
HMG Nest	24"/60cm	6	2	6	ROF 3 when pinned down.

Lafayette, We Are Here
MEUSE-ARGONNE OFFENSIVE

When the Untied Stated finally went to war in April of 1917 its Army was not prepared to meet the challenges that awaited it on the battlefields of Europe. What America did have, which the rest of their allies lacked, was a source of manpower that seemed inexhaustible. Under the command of General John 'Black Jack' Pershing, the American Expeditionary Force (AEF) raised an army of over 4 million men and was able to get half of that number sent to France by the time the war ended. The lack of suitable material was solved by borrowing heavy weapons and artillery from the French and British, who also trained their new allies in the ways of modern trench warfare.

The Americans finally got into the fight in October of 1917 seeing action all over the Western Front, and notably stopped the final German offensive from reaching Paris in the battles of Château-Thierry and Belleau Wood in the summer of 1918. After the success of the Americans in these battles, Pershing lobbied hard for the AEF to be an independent American command in the field as opposed to being broken up and given piecemeal to the French and British armies as manpower to bolster worn out units already in the front line.

Having won his fight for a separate force, Pershing led the AEF into the offenses of St Mihel, and the hard fought Meuse-Argonne campaign. The influx of the fresh AEF came about as the manpower of the Allies was nearly drained and greatly contributed to the defeat of Imperial Germany.

US Tanks and Patton

The most iconic individual that is forever tied to the tank in the US Army did not begin his career as a tanker. George Patton, who would rise to four-star General in the Second World War and be known as the 'Father of US Armor', went overseas in 1917 as a member of General Pershing's staff. Captain Patton soon grew bored in his position of overseeing the training for the US troops arriving in France. It was during this time Patton first saw the tank and thought about what it could bring to the battlefield.

Patton volunteered to set up the first ever tank school in the US Army. Using Renault tanks borrowed from the French, Patton soon put his new trainees to work learning how to use this new weapon. Patton's work in training his new tankers paid off and he was given command of the 1st Provisional Tank Brigade, which he personally took into combat during the St Mihiel offensive in September 1918.

Meuse-Argonne Offensive

In what is known as the single largest battle in US Army history, the Meuse-Argonne Offensive saw over 1.2 million doughboys go into action as a part of the series of combined Allied offenses intended to smash the German army in the field and bring about the end of the war.

After successfully lobbying the other Allied leaders for an independent American Army, General John Pershing looked

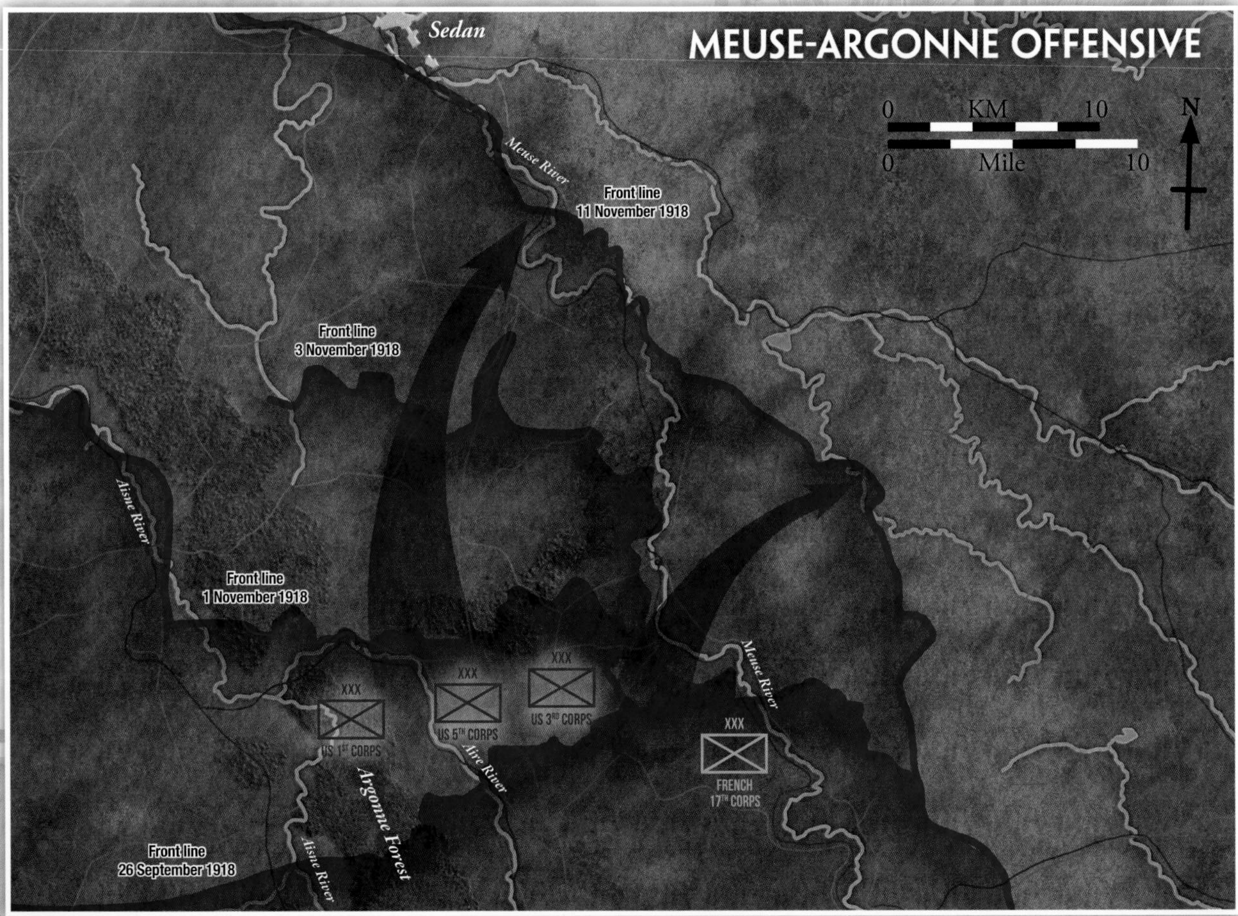

for opportunities where the AEF could be used in the offensive role.

The first test for the Americans was the battle to reduce the salient around St Mihiel France in September 1918. This successful battle saw the first use of US tank units in combat and the first large scale use of US airpower in support of the AEF.

Pershing didn't let the AEF rest on the laurels of St Mihiel very long, and soon went about undertaking a massive shift of US forces to the Meuse-Argonne sector of the line. Overseeing this move of an entire American army was a little known staff officer named George C. Marshall, who knew he had to move hundreds of thousands of men, guns, tanks, and supplies northwards in a short amount of time. Kicking off 11 days after the end of the St Mihiel offensive, the Meuse-Argonne offensive started 26 Oct 1918, when the AEF attacked the German lines heading northwards towards their objective of Sedan.

While many US units were able to achieve their assignments during the opening of the battle, the deep forest benefited the German units who were left to defend the sector, inflicting massive losses and confusion among many American units still new to combat. It was in this offensive that the 'Lost Battalion' and Sergeant (actually a Corporal at the time) Alvin York became known, as well as a simple battery commander from Missouri, Captain Harry S. Truman.

Despite the losses, Pershing pushed the American units to keep on attacking, knowing that they had to keep the pressure on the Germans all along the front line. For 47 straight days, US divisions rotated into the front lines in what could be best described as frontal attacks reminiscent of 1914, and paid heavily for their advances. The poor roads of the Argonne forest, combined with the bad weather created massive traffic jams that made supporting each attack nearly impossible. Even with these limitations, Pershing kept pushing the AEF to renew its thrust until it would reach the heights overlooking Sedan just before the end of the war. It was said that German General Paul von Hindenburg remarked that the size and determination of the American attacks in the Argonne decided the war for the allies.

It was in this battle that the American Army went from newcomers to crafty veterans. With each minor victory or setback, American soldiers, from General Pershing to the lowest doughboy, learned the hard lessons of war and what it took to succeed in battle. The American Army that came out of the Meuse-Argonne was bloodied, but was a battle hardened force that had learned how to win on the modern combined-force battlefield of the 20th Century.

AMERICAN SPECIAL RULES

An American Rifle Company does not use any of the US special rules found in the Flames Of War rulebook, and instead uses Quick Fire (see page 37) and the following special rules.

Over There

Commanders of the American forces in France were determined that they should be treated as equals, and not parcelled out and used to fill gaps by their Allies. The American soldiers proved to be capable and brave. They did not let their commanders down, showing valiant conduct under fire and a willingness to press home attacks.

Any American Platoon that is Pinned Down may re-roll failed Motivation tests to rally from being Pinned Down or remount vehicles after being Bailed Out.

The famous Uncle Sam recruitment poster was made by J. M. Flagg in 1917. Over four million copies of the poster were printed during World War I, and it was revived for World War II.

Sergeant York

American platoons had good NCOs that they followed into combat no matter what.

An American platoon may Charge into Combat and Consolidate without having a Platoon Command team, and if it does so, the Assaulting teams do not need to be or remain In Command.

Lafayette, We Are Here

The arrival of the Americans was a great boost to the French soldiers morale. The Americans' good will, enthusiasm, and quality of their equipment did much to lift the spirits of the French *Poilu*.

French platoons in an American force to do not count as Allied Platoons (See page 70 of the rulebook).

Trench Fighters

Learning quickly from their Allies, by 1918 the Americans had adopted the methods of attack developed by the British and French in the hard fought years of 1916 and 1917.

Rifle and Pistol teams from American Rifle Platoons (page 48) hit on a roll of 2+ in Assaults if they are Veterans (instead of 3+) or 3+ if they are Trained (instead of 4+).

VB and MG teams support the assault from behind the charge and therefore do not benefit from the Trench Fighters special rule.

Rifle Company

Infantry Company

You must field one platoon from each box shaded black and may field one platoon from each box shaded grey.

Your Company HQ must be either 1st Infantry Division (marked) or 42nd Infantry Division (marked). All Platoons with these symbols must be the same division as your Company HQ.

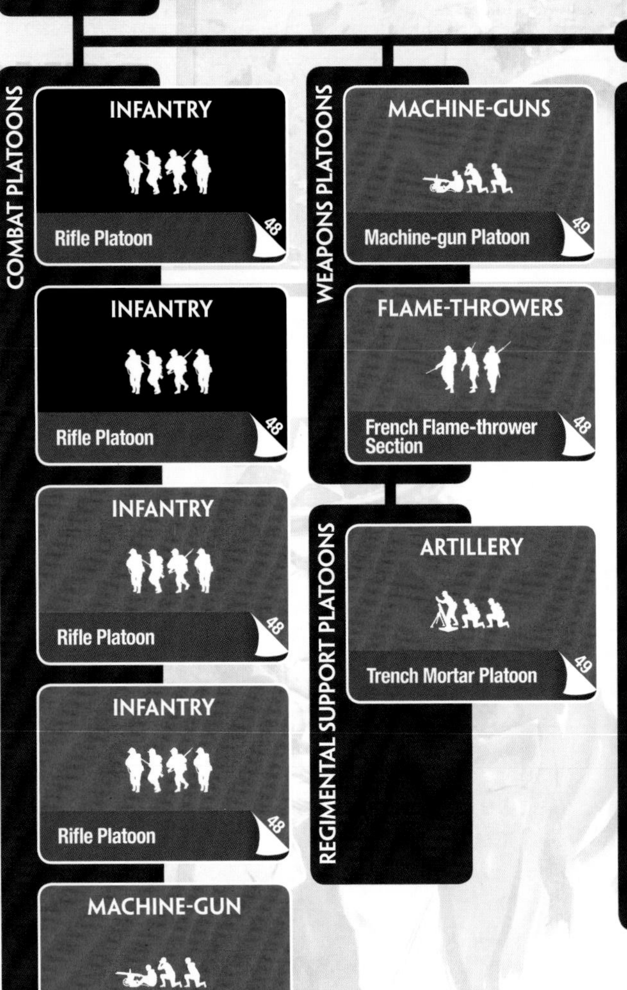

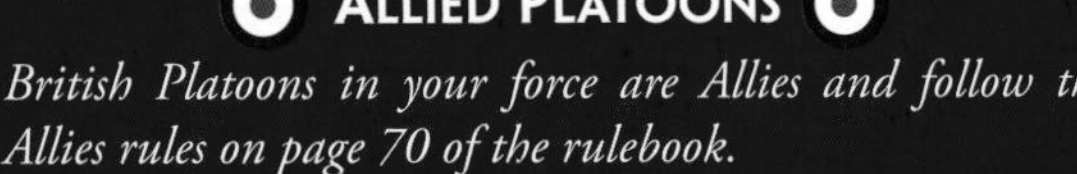

Allied Platoons

British Platoons in your force are Allies and follow the Allies rules on page 70 of the rulebook.

Motivation and Skill

A 1st Infantry Division Rifle Company is rated as **Confident Veteran.**

A 42nd Infantry Division Rifle Company s is rated as **Confident Trained.**

1st Infantry	
Reluctant	Conscript
Confident	Trained
Fearless	**Veteran**

42nd Infantry	
Reluctant	Conscript
Confident	**Trained**
Fearless	Veteran

Headquarters

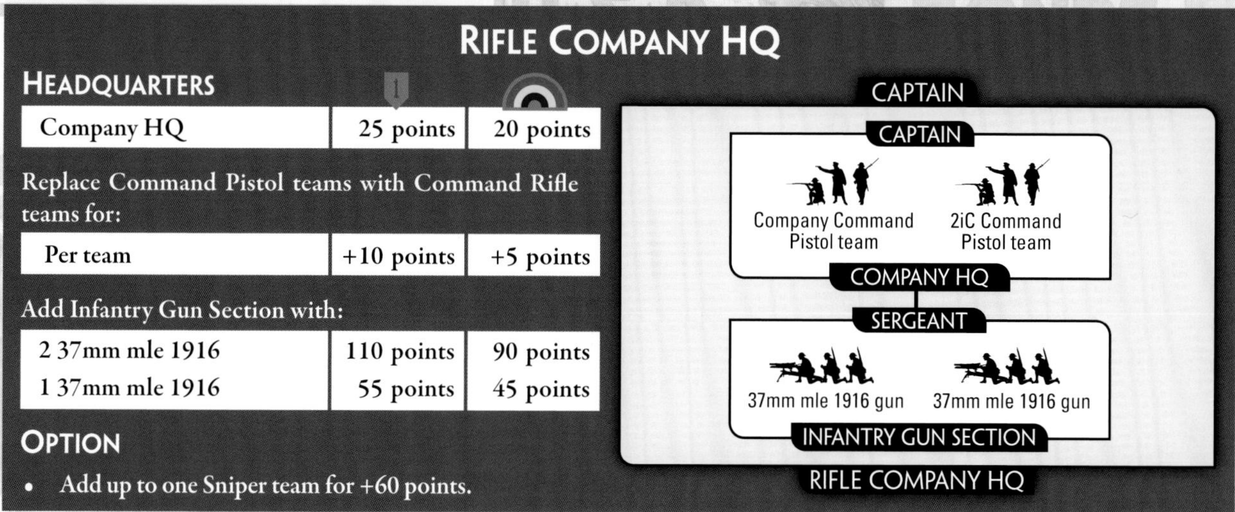

Rifle Company HQ

Headquarters

	1st	42nd
Company HQ	25 points	20 points

Replace Command Pistol teams with Command Rifle teams for:

Per team	+10 points	+5 points

Add Infantry Gun Section with:

2 37mm mle 1916	110 points	90 points
1 37mm mle 1916	55 points	45 points

Option

- Add up to one Sniper team for +60 points.

Having been trained by our allies in trench warfare we are ready to take our place in the line alongside the *Poilu* and Tommy to push the Germans out of France. Our French allies have given us the excellent 37mm mle 1916 trench gun, equally effective against tanks and pillboxes.

1st and 42nd Infantry Divisions

No two units can better illustrate the diversity of the AEF than the 1st and 42nd Infantry divisions. When the US declared war on Germany in 1917 the army was not prepared to adequately mobilize an army of what would become over four million men in size. The regular US Army was small and not even organized into divisions until 1917. The US did have a large National Guard, which consisted of part time soldiers, most of whom never served in the regular military. Adding to these formations was the thousands of volunteers who enlisted right after the declaration of war and the draftees, after conscription was started in June of 1917.

When the US finally formed divisions, they were huge by European standards. The Square formation of these units had two brigades each with two regiments. Each division having about 28,000 men, these formations were twice the size of the paper strength of any British, French, or even German division on the Western Front.

The Big Red One

The 1st US Infantry Division, formed in 1917, was the first unit sent over to France during the Great War. The Big Red One was cobbled together from four regular army regiments based throughout the United States. The men who made up the Big Red One were veterans of many years of active service with some seeing combat in Mexico and the Philippines in the years prior to the Great War. The division was one of the first to train with the British and French and was part of the first US victory in the war, the battle of Cantigny. The division acquitted itself well in combat, seeing action in every major battle the US fought in and even today it adds to its legacy being the oldest serving division in the US Army.

The Rainbow Division

Formed in 1917, the 42nd Infantry Division was formed by taking the best National Guard units from 26 different states. The fact it combined troops from all over the country caused its Chief of Staff, Colonel Douglas MacArthur to comment that the unit 'would stretch over the entire country like a rainbow'. With other National Guard divisions being from a specific region, the Rainbow Division had a unique flavour and even combined men from both the north and south, units that were at war with one another a half century before in the US Civil War. During the war the Rainbow Division was placed under both French and US command and was committed to combat for 264 days. After playing a major role in the St Mihiel and Meuse-Argonne campaigns the unit returned to the US and was deactivated. The 42nd was once again called to serve in the Second World War, and even today serves as a National Guard Division, combining troops from 14 states in the northeastern United States.

The Big Red One and the Rainbow Division well represent the Doughboys who made up the American Expeditionary Force in the Great War.

COMBAT PLATOONS

Rifle Platoon

Platoon

2 Rifle Half-Platoons each with:		
2 Rifle Squads	420 points	320 points
1 Rifle Half-Platoon with:		
2 Rifle Squads	210 points	160 points

Rifle Half-Platoons operate as separate platoons, each with their own command team.

Our platoons number twice the size of both our battle worn allies and enemy. Split into half platoons, our light machine gun squads with either Lewis or Chauchat machine guns can keep the enemies heads down while our rifle squads close in. If we encounter any enemy machine gun nests our Vivien and Bessières rifle grenades can quickly take them out.

WEAPONS PLATOONS

French Flame-thrower Section

Platoon

3 Flame-thrower teams	120 points	90 points
2 Flame-thrower teams	80 points	60 points
1 Flame-thrower team	40 points	30 points

A French Flame-thrower Section must make Combat Attachments to US Rifle Half-Platoons with all of their teams. Flame-thrower teams my be distributed among any US Rifle Half-Platoons or attached to a single platoon.

SERGENT

SERGENT

Flame-thrower team Flame-thrower team Flame-thrower team

FLAME-THROWER SECTION

FRENCH FLAME-THROWER SECTION

Modern warfare is deadly and requires weapons that can terrorize our enemies. Our French allies are here to support us with one such weapon, the Flame-thrower. These deadly weapons will make any German lurking in cover think twice about fighting.

Machine-gun Platoon

Platoon

HQ Section with:

4 Hotchkiss mle 1914 HMG	290 points	225 points
3 Hotchkiss mle 1914 HMG	220 points	170 points
2 Hotchkiss mle 1914 HMG	150 points	115 points

In addition, a Machine-gun Platoon may fire bombardments (see page 4).

With the machine-gun ruling no man's land we are lucky to have the French Hotchkiss mle 1914 heavy machine gun to call on for support. Either beating back a German attack or providing a machine gun bombardment for our advancing troops we have one of the best machine guns available.

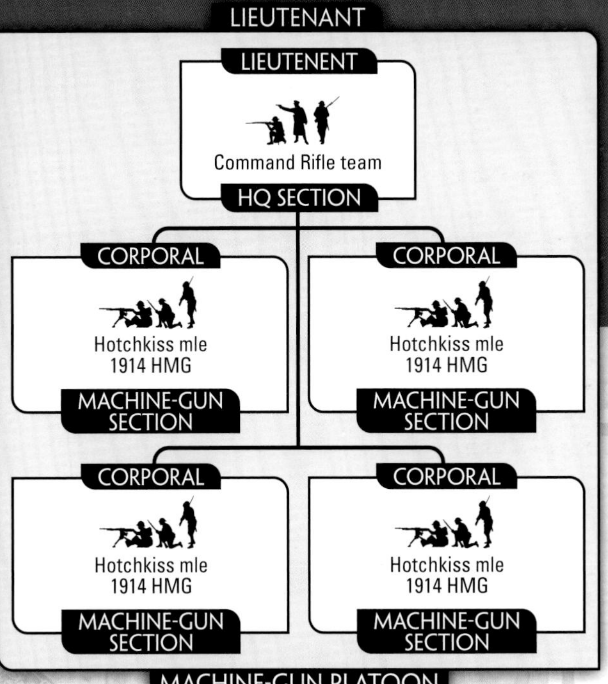

REGIMENTAL SUPPORT PLATOONS

Trench Mortar Platoon

Platoon

HQ Section with:

4 3" Stokes	360 points	280 points
3 3" Stokes	270 points	210 points
2 3" Stokes	180 points	140 points
1 3" Stokes	90 points	70 points
4 58mm Type 2	420 points	320 points
3 58mm Type 2	315 points	240 points
2 58mm Type 2	210 points	160 points
1 58mm Type 2	105 points	80 points

LIEUTENANT

LIEUTENANT — Command Mortar — MORTAR SECTION

SERGEANT — Command Mortar — MORTAR SECTION

CORPORAL — Command Mortar — MORTAR SECTION

CORPORAL — Command Mortar — MORTAR SECTION

TRENCH MORTAR PLATOON

Mortar Sections operate as separate platoons, each gun is their own Command team.

3" Stokes and 58mm Type 2 mortar teams are Trench Guns (see page 4).

Both our allies have provided us with trench mortars to deal with enemy pillboxes, nests, or strongpoints. The British 3" Stokes mortar can advance with our troops, while the heavier French 58mm Type 2 mortar can stay in the rear, knocking out any points of resistance we may face.

DIVISIONAL SUPPORT PLATOONS

ARTILLERY BATTERY

PLATOON

HQ Section with:

4 75mm mle 1897	710 points	545 points
2 75mm mle 1897	360 points	275 points

OPTION

- Add horse-drawn limbers for +5 points for the platoon.

A Rifle Company that includes an Artillery Battery will Always Defend.

Despite its age, our 75mm mle 1897 guns are one of the best support weapons around. Known affectionately as the *soixante-quinze*, this ground breaking design of the 19th Century can provide rapid fire support for our doughboys and take on any German armour we may run up against. The high rate of fire of the *soixante-quinze* sets it apart from the guns used by the British and the Huns across no-man's land.

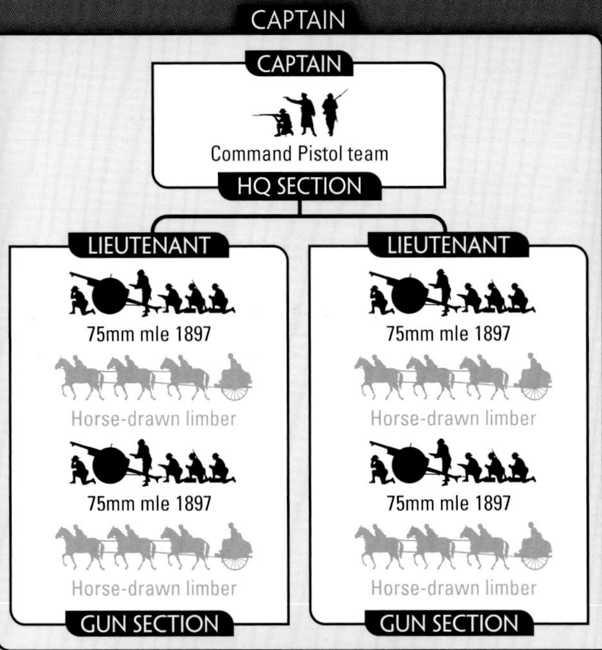

ARTILLERY DETACHMENT

PLATOON

2 75mm mle 1897	340 points	260 points
1 75mm mle 1897	170 points	130 points

OPTION

- Add horse-drawn limbers for +5 points for the battery.

Each Gun Section operates as separate platoon, each guns is their own Command team.

LIEUTENANT

SERGEANT
Command 75mm mle 1897
Horse-drawn limber
GUN SECTION

ARTILLERY DETACHMENT

LIGHT TANK PLATOON

PLATOON

HQ Section with:

3 Renault FT-17 (37mm) and 2 Renault FT-17 (MG)	565 points
2 Renault FT-17 (37mm) and 2 Renault FT-17 (MG)	440 points
2 Renault FT-17 (37mm) and 1 Renault FT-17 (MG)	345 points
1 Renault FT-17 (37mm) and 1 Renault FT-17 (MG)	220 points

While they sound like a tractor from back home, these US tanks, the first we have ever had can spearhead an attack and take on the tough German defences. Borrowed from the French, the Renault FT-17 represents the latest innovation in tank technology. Its two man crew can operate a machine gun or a 37mm cannon as it charges through the barbed wire of no-man's land.

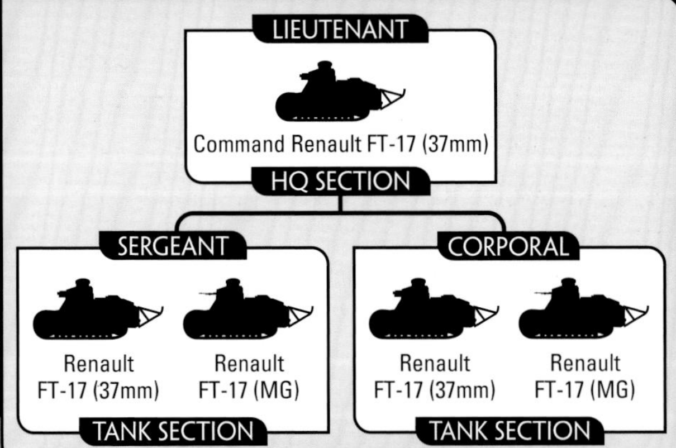

A Light Tank Platoon is rated **Confident Trained.**

CONFIDENT | TRAINED

American Arsenal

TANK TEAMS

Name *Weapon*	Mobility *Range*	Armour Front *ROF*	 Side *Anti-tank*	 Top *Firepower*	Equipment and Notes
TANKS					
Renault FT-17 (MG)	6"/15cm	1	1	1	Overloaded, Turret MG.
Renault FT-17 (37mm)	6"/15cm	1	1	1	Overloaded.
37mm SA-18 gun	*16"/40cm*	*2*	*4*	*4+*	*One-man turret.*

GUN TEAMS

Weapon	Mobility	Range	ROF	Anti-tank	Firepower	Notes
Hotchkiss mle 1914 HMG	Man-packed	24"/60cm	6	2	6	ROF 3 when pinned down or moving.
Firing bombardments		40"/100cm	-	-	-	
3" Stokes mortar	Light	24"/60cm	2	2	3+	Can fire over friendly teams, Minimum range 8"/20cm, Trench gun.
58mm Type 2 mortar	Medium	32"/80cm	2	2	2+	Can fire over friendly teams, Minimum range 8"/20cm, Trench gun.
37mm mle 1916 gun	Man-packed	16"/40cm	3	4	4+	
75mm mle 1897 gun	Heavy	24"/60cm	2	8	3+	Gun shield, Quick fire.
Firing bombardments		64"/160cm	-	3	6	

INFANTRY TEAMS

Team	Range	ROF	Anti-tank	Firepower	Notes
Pistol team	4"/10cm	2	1	6	Full ROF when moving, Trench fighters.
Rifle team	16"/40cm	1	2	6	Trench fighters.
MG team	16"/40cm	3	2	6	ROF 2 when pinned downs.
VB team	8"/20cm	2	1	4+	Can fire over friendly teams.
Flame-thrower team	4"/10cm	2	-	6	Flame-thrower.

TRANSPORT TEAMS

Vehicle *Weapon*	Mobility *Range*	Front *ROF*	Armour Side *Anti-tank*	 Top *Firepower*	Equipment and Notes
TRACTORS					
Horse-drawn limber	Horse-drawn	-	-	-	

FORTIFICATIONS

BUNKERS AND PILLBOXES

Weapon	Range	ROF	Anti-tank	Firepower	Notes
HMG Pillbox	24"/60cm	6	2	6	ROF 3 when pinned down.
HMG Nest	24"/60cm	6	2	6	ROF 3 when pinned down.

IRON FORTRESSES
BRITISH, GERMAN, AND FRENCH TANKS OF WWI

The First World War was, more than anything, characterized by the grim reality of advanced military technology coupled with outdated military tactics. Open ground infantry engagements which had characterized so many previous European conflicts were obsolete in 1914 because of the rapid advances in integrated defensive systems. Barbed wire was cheap, easy to erect in multiple layers, and created a formidable barrier for advancing infantry. When combined with trench systems, reliable machine-guns, and modern artillery, infantry attacking in the open suffered horrific casualties. The end result was that neither side could mount an effective offensive creating a prolonged stalemate on the Western Front through 1917.

New weapons and tactics would therefore be required to achieve any sort of breakthrough. While senior commanders on both sides of the conflict failed to predict that the Great War would bog down into static trench warfare, there were some visionaries that recognized the danger and began work on solutions.

In August 1914, the French Colonel Jean Baptiste Eugène Estienne predicted that, '…victory will belong … to the one of the two belligerents who will be the first to succeed in mounting a 75 mm gun on a vehicle capable of moving in all types of terrain.' Initially the various forces experimented with various armoured cars, and while these worked well on roads or hard terrain, they had several drawbacks in mobility and their light construction made addition of heavy armour or armament impossible.

In October 1914, British Lieutenant-Colonel Ernest Swinton suggested that using vehicles with caterpillar tracks, rather than wheels, would both improve mobility and could carry more weight. They could be fitted with enough weaponry and armour to break through enemy trench systems.

Enter the Royal Navy

Swinton was unable to obtain army backing for the project as their early tests with a caterpillar-equipped Holt tractor were unsatisfactory. However, a certain member of the Committee of Imperial Defence, saw potential in the idea. Winston Churchill was First Lord of the Admiralty, and he was determined to move forward with the idea, even if it meant exceeding his authority.

British efforts to develop an effective armoured vehicle took time because of the army's disinterest and major British industrial players not wanting to get involved.

Despite these handicaps, in 1915, the Landships Committee, as it became to be known, developed a set of requirements which called for trench-crossing ability, speed, basic armour, and its minimum armament. The committee also gave these new vehicles a codename: 'tanks', pretending to be developing a self-propelled water tank in order to camouflage the role the vehicle was intended to play.

First Prototypes

'Little Willie' was the first British vehicle developed incorporating caterpillar tracks and a large box superstructure. Unfortunately the commercial tracks used were not up to the task, and a new track system was developed.

The next design, known as 'Big Willie' or 'Mother', was developed by Lieutenant Walter Gordon Wilson and incorporated the rhomboidal shape characteristic of many British tanks of World War I. Trials on the new vehicle were completed by 2 February 1916, and by 12 February an order for 100 vehicles (later expanded to 150) was placed.

The Tank Goes to War

Reaching action in mid-September 1916, early results with the Mark I were promising, especially when the tanks were used in groups. Several shortcomings were evident in the Mark I, so an improved version, the Mark IV, was developed.

One of the key improvements was an increase in armour thickness to provide proof against German armour-piercing bullets. The naval six pounders used on the Mark I were also

replaced with a shorter six pounder as the longer guns tended to bury their muzzles in mud and the barrels bent more easily than army equivalents.

The Mark IV

Improvements were also made to the armour and armament. The Mark IV tank incorporated several automotive and structural improvements. One of the key characteristics of the British rhomboidal tanks was the primary armament being carried in external sponsons on both sides of the tank.

In previous marks, these sponsons were fixed and had to be removed to transport the vehicle by rail. Given that each sponson weighed over a ton, removal and reattachment were arduous tasks. The Mark IV's sponsons were, however, retractable saving a great deal of time.

To ensure the vehicle wouldn't stall at steep angles of attack, the gravity fuel feed of the Mark I was replaced with a vacuum system. The final drive was also enclosed based on experience with the Mark I.

Its six-cylinder Daimler engine provided 105hp giving the 28-ton vehicle a top speed of about 4mph. The vehicle required a very large crew of eight to man the various armaments and control the vehicle. Simply steering the vehicle required the coordinated effort of four crewmen: the driver, two gearsmen, and the commander. The driver controlled the primary gearbox, the gearsmen controlled the high/low gear ratios separately on each track, and the commander controlled the brakes. Reverse gear was controlled by the driver, but the gear ratio was set fairly high resulting in poor reverse performance for the vehicle, making it difficult for the Mark IV to un-ditch itself.

The Mark IV was produced in two major variants, 420 'male' tanks which carried two six pounder guns and three Lewis .303 machine guns, and 595 'female' tanks, in which the six-pounder guns were replaced with two additional Lewis machine guns.

Later in the war, as a result of combat experience in tank versus tank combat, some Mark IV female tanks had one of their machine gun sponsons replaced with a six-pounder sponson creating a Mark IV 'hermaphrodite'.

In addition to the combat tanks, over 200 tank tenders with boosted engines were built to carry tank supplies. These tenders had square mild steel sponsons which easily distinguished them from the combat tanks.

Cambrai

Tanks had been used with mixed success through 1917 and the development of effective armoured tactics had been slow to develop. It was not until the Battle of Cambrai, in late November 1917, that the higher echelons of the British command were convinced of the utility of this new weapon.

Though not the first use of combined arms, Cambrai was one of the more effective employments of armour in conjunction with infantry and artillery allowing the Allied armies to advance more than five miles. The advance included over 400

British tanks, largely Mark IVs. Unfortunately little in the way of reserves was available to secure the captured ground and a German counteroffensive quickly retook the lost ground. The success of the initial advance, however, provided the political impetus needed for continued support of the armoured forces

THE WHIPPET

While the Mark I and later the Mark IV tanks were excellent infantry support weapons, and could even create a substantial breach in an enemy line when used in numbers, they lacked the speed to exploit that gap. In late 1916, William Tritton proposed a faster vehicle to the Landships Committee which would be capable of filling this role on the battlefield.

The new vehicle, called the Medium Mark A or 'Whippet', was a radical departure from the heavier rhomboidal tanks. The caterpillar tracks, derived from the Little Willie prototype, were more conventional side-slung units as opposed to the all-around tracks of the Mark IV.

Though originally envisioned with a rotating turret, the production model had an armoured housing for three to four .303 Hotchkiss machine guns (though most were fitted with two guns), which could be relocated between four gun ports. Approved in June 1917, roughly 200 vehicles were produced starting in October 1917.

Unlike the large crew of the Mark IV, the Whippet managed with a standard crew of three, a commander, driver, and gunner. Given the gunner was responsible for manning both machine guns (which could point forward, left, right, and rear), sometimes a second gunner was squeezed in.

As its primary role was to get these guns into the enemy rear as quickly as possible, the Whippet was designed with two 45hp engines-one powering each track. This gave the Whippet a top speed of 8.3 mph, far faster than its heavier cousins.

The Whippet reached the battlefield during the British Army's low ebb following crippling 1918 losses in Flanders. Their first action was to cover the retreat of British infantry during the German Spring Offensive. The machine-gun armament of the Whippet proved devastating to infantry caught in the open of no-man's land, with seven Whippets effectively halting two German infantry battalions at an engagement near Cachy and Villers-Brettoneux.

GERMANY'S TANK

The Germans began exploring the possibility of developing their own armoured vehicles soon after the first encounter with British tanks in September 1916. However, the process was slow and clearly had lower priority than the British and French efforts.

The A7V committee oversaw development of a German-designed tank, and by the end of October 1916 they had developed the specifications for the tank. The initial design and plans were completed by December 1916, but were revised in February 1917 to incorporate the updated specification of 30mm of frontal armour plate.

The resulting A7V tank was a 24' by 10' (7.3m x 3m) box with two track units slung beneath the fighting compartment. Armour thickness was 30mm on the front, 15mm on the sides, and 20mm on the rear. Armament consisted of one 5.7cm Maxim-Nordenfelt gun facing front and a total of six Maxim machine guns arrayed around the sides and rear.

Two 100hp four-cylinder engines powered the tank giving the vehicle a reasonable power to weight ratio for the time. The caterpillar track system of the A7V also had one key advantage over its Allied contemporaries-the A7V utilized a spring loaded suspension system rather than the crude un-sprung systems found on Allied tanks. This gave the A7V a speed of roughly 8 mph on flat ground, making the German

MARK A MEDIUM 'WHIPPET'

Top Armour: 1 | Side Armour: 1 | Movement: 8"/20cm | Front Armour: 1

Weapon	Range	ROF	AT	FP
two Lewis MG, each:	16"/40cm	3	2	6

A7V

Top Armour: 1 | Side Armour: 1 | Movement: 6"/15cm | Front Armour: 2

Landship, Overloaded, Self-defence MG

Weapon	Range	ROF	AT	FP
5.7cm Maxim-Nordenfelt gun	24"/60cm	2	6	4+
six Maxim MG, each:	16"/40cm	3	3	6

heavy tank roughly as quick as the British Whippet or nearly twice as fast as the Mark IV.

As with all early tanks, the A7V had its share of problems. The engines tended to overheat and were difficult to start, the gearboxes were fragile, the tracks were weak, and even the armour plate had severe variations in strength and thickness. The A7V required a crew of 18 to operate properly, though 12 members of the crew were responsible for the six machine guns in two man teams. Trench-crossing ability and ground clearance were inferior to many of the Allied tanks resulting in the A7V frequently bogging down in soft terrain.

Production of the A7V tanks was painfully slow. Although the Germans placed an order for 100 vehicles, the first vehicle was not delivered until 1 October 1917. By the end of the war only 20 were produced requiring the Germans to rely on captured British and French tanks for much of their armoured strength.

A7V IN COMBAT

The A7V first saw combat on 21 March 1918 where *1. Abteilung* (or ATD 1) stopped a British advance with three A7V.

Perhaps the most famous engagement involving the A7V was on 24 April 1918 at the Second Battle of Villers-Bretonneux. Three British Mark IV tanks (one male and two female) engaged a total of three German A7V tanks in history's first tank versus tank engagement. The A7V 'Nixe' (mermaid) engaged the Mark IV female tanks and heavily damaged them with its 57mm gun. As their machine guns were ineffective against the German tanks' armour, the female tanks limped away.

The remaining Male tank (interestingly Number 1 tank of Number 1 section of A Company of the British 1st Battalion) opened fire on the German behemoth with its six pounders disabling it. With its crew in retreat, the male was joined by several Whippet tanks and engaged the supporting German infantry and the two A7V.

In the face of these superior numbers, the A7V withdrew to the safety of their lines. They returned once German artillery disabled the male. The A7Vs engaged the Whippets and destroyed a couple before the British tanks quit the field. All of the tanks were later recovered by their respective sides.

SECURING A LEGACY

Despite their numerous mechanical and design shortcomings, the tanks of World War I proved a valuable asset in breaking the trench stalemate which had dominated warfare on the Western Front for years. It is interesting to note that while the A7V and Mark IV tanks were rendered quickly technologically obsolete shortly after the war, the Whippet soldiered for decades in the armed forces of other nations. Some were in use by the Imperial Japanese Army in Manchuria in the early 1930s.

While the early tanks were not decisive on their own, the tank had proved itself on the field of battle as an indispensable component of modern combined arms warfare.

FRENCH TANKS

Like the Germans and the British, the French also looked at the tank as a means to break the deadlock on the western front. In spite of the fact that the British were allied to France, each nation developed tank designs independently. However, they shared the idea that a tracked vehicle would be the best basis for a design. The first prototype designed by the French Schneider company used American Holt tractors as the chassis which supported an armored box where the crew and armament would be located. This first design became known as the Schneider CA.1, and the French had about 400 models of the CA.1 built from February 1916 until the end of the war.

Around the same time as the CA.1 was being tested, an advocate for the tank emerged from the ranks of the French army. Jean Baptiste Eugène Estienne, a colonel with a background in artillery saw the first tests of the CA.1 and became convinced of the potential of this new weapon and immediately championed the project. In 1916 Estienne was put in charge of creating the new tank arm in the French military. He set about recruiting tank crews, developing tank training, and establishing the first units equipped with tanks. In April 1917, the top French commander Robert Nivelle, ordered Estienne to attack the German lines near Berry-au-Bac. The attack was premature and the French tankers suffered heavily. However, Estienne continued to train his force and advocate for newer and better tanks for his new force.

Estienne had some influence on the next French heavy tank, the Saint Chamond. The Saint Chamond was much like the previous CA.1, in which a heavy armored box was mounted to a tracked chassis. However the weight of the Saint Chamond required a powerful engine, which the French did not put in the Saint Chamond, leaving it very under powered and ill-suited for use in the trenches.

The final French design of the war was the Renault FT-17, which was seen as a major leap forward in tank design. This small tank featured a rotating turret, which became a mainstay of tank design thereafter. The FT-17 featured a two man crew and an engine and chassis that could easily navigate the torn ground of no-man's land and the trenches. The design was so successful that the FT-17 saw service all over the world for many different nations and was even around at the start of the Second World War.

The French really embraced the idea of the tank and by the end of the war, they had built almost 4,000 tanks of all models, easily building more than the British and Germans combined.

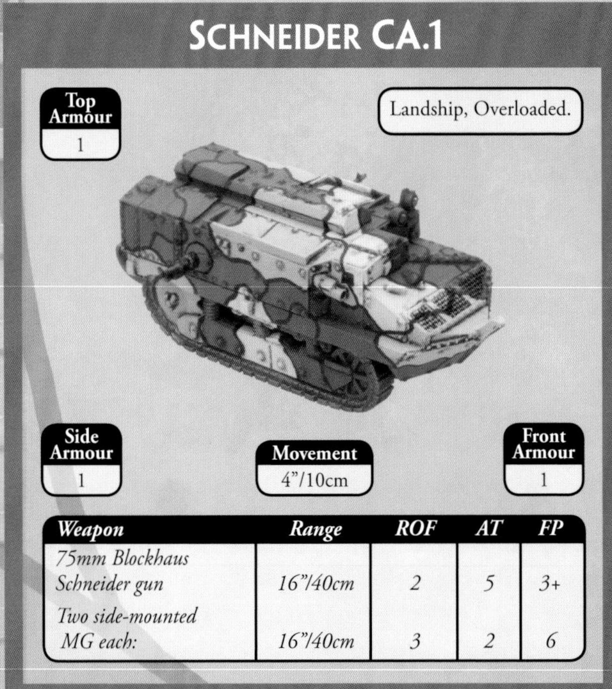

SCHNEIDER CA.1

Top Armour: 1

Landship, Overloaded.

Side Armour: 1

Movement: 4"/10cm

Front Armour: 1

Weapon	*Range*	*ROF*	*AT*	*FP*
75mm Blockhaus Schneider gun	*16"/40cm*	*2*	*5*	*3+*
Two side-mounted MG each:	*16"/40cm*	*3*	*2*	*6*

SCHNEIDER CA.1

This first design of a heavy tank weighed about 13.6 tons and was armed with a short 75mm cannon, and two Hotchkiss machine guns. The crew of 6 worked in a very cramped space, and the tank's layout was very poor, having its sole 75mm gun on the right side of the tank and had a poor field of vision. The 60 hp Schneider gasoline engine of the CA.1 gave the tank a top speed of 8.1 kph (5 mph); however it normally moved at 2-3 kph due to the difficulty of driving the CA.1. While not the best designed French tank of the war, the CA.1 was used until the final battles in 1918.

SAINT CHAMOND

France's second attempt at designing a heavy tank led to the Saint Chamond, which was the largest tank built in France during the war. Weighing in at 23 tones, the Saint Chamond was armed with a full size 75mm gun located in the front of the vehicle, with 4 Hotchkiss machine guns located on the sides. The eight man crew had to squeeze into the hull of the tank which was only a little bigger than the 6-man CA.1. While its power plant could move the vehicle at 12 kph, its extended overhanging front hull tended to drive into the ground leaving the Saint Chamond bogged down in the rough terrain of the front lines. France produced about 400 of the Saint Chamond tanks during the war and used them alongside their other designs until the armistice in 1918.

RENAULT FT-17

For French tank design the third time was the charm, and the result was the game changing Renault FT-17. The FT-17 was a huge departure from previous designs as it was much smaller than the CA.1 and the Saint Chamond, and featured a two man crew. It also had the first rotating turret that enabled the Commander/Gunner to fire its 37mm gun or Hotchkiss machine gun 360 degrees, allowing them to engage any target nearby. Using a car engine, these super light tanks were only able to move at 10 kph (6 mph), and were designed to be used in mass formations working with the infantry to eliminate enemy pockets of resistance. Other nations adopted the FT-17, and it became the standard tank used by the Americans during the war. By the end of the war, the French had built almost 3000 FT-17s and continued production of the tank with very little modification until the 1930's.

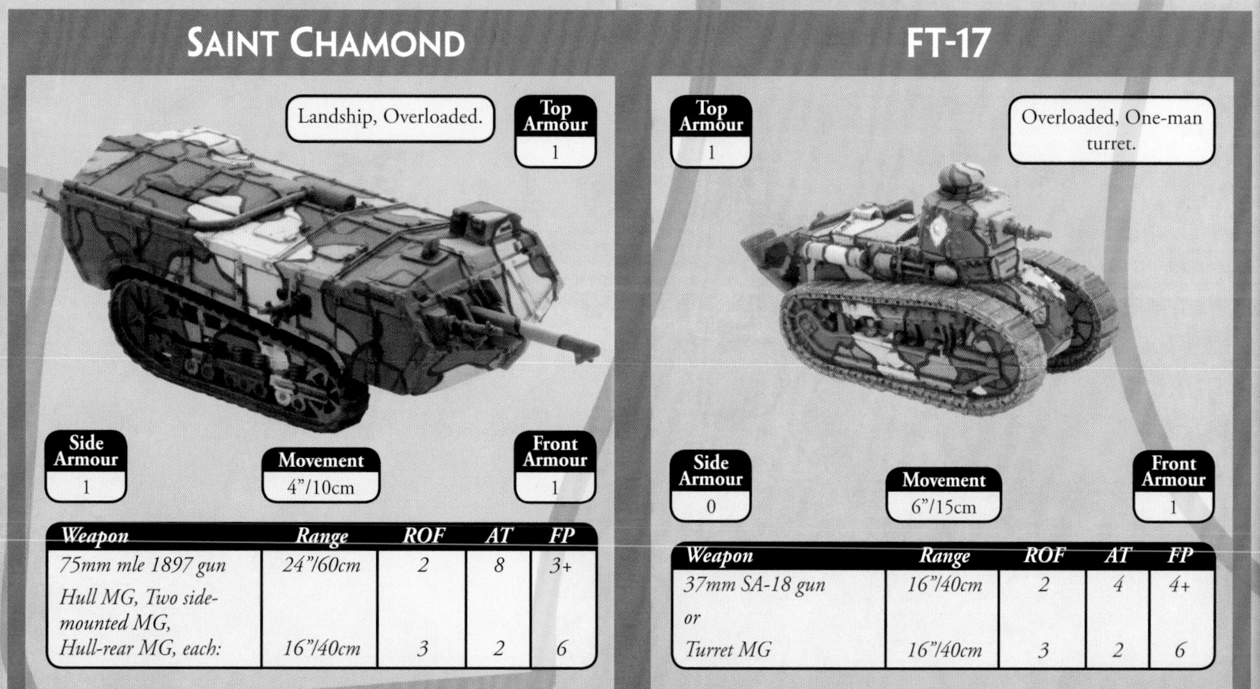

SAINT CHAMOND

Landship, Overloaded.

Top Armour: 1 | Side Armour: 1 | Movement: 4"/10cm | Front Armour: 1

Weapon	Range	ROF	AT	FP
75mm mle 1897 gun	*24"/60cm*	2	8	3+
Hull MG, Two side-mounted MG, Hull-rear MG, each:	*16"/40cm*	3	2	6

FT-17

Overloaded, One-man turret.

Top Armour: 1 | Side Armour: 0 | Movement: 6"/15cm | Front Armour: 1

Weapon	Range	ROF	AT	FP
37mm SA-18 gun	*16"/40cm*	2	4	4+
or				
Turret MG	*16"/40cm*	3	2	6

GREAT WAR MISSIONS

MISSION SPECIAL RULES

PRELIMINARY BOMBARDMENT

Before a major attack the defender is subjected to a bombardment from every gun and howitzer available.

All defending platoons on the table start the game Pinned Down.

CRATERED GROUND

Bombardments often leave the battlefront a moonscape of cratered ground.

Stationary Infantry and Man-packed Gun teams count as in Bullet-proof Cover while in Cratered terrain.

OVERWHELMING FORCE

An assault company can rely on the rest of their battalion following up to push further into the trenches.

When an Attacking platoon that is entirely made up of Infantry or Man-packed Gun teams is Destroyed, the Attacker may return it to play at the start of their next turn, representing a fresh platoon arriving to take over.

In the Starting Step after an Attacking platoon is Destroyed, but before Company Morale Checks, the platoon may be returned to play. The returning platoon is deployed anywhere in the Attacker's Deployment Area.

The new platoon starts at the original strength of the Destroyed platoon. Only teams that are actually part of the platoon return in the new platoon. All Attachments, Warriors, and Independent Teams Destroyed with the platoon are permanently lost and do not return.

You do not need to wait for an Attacking platoon to be Destroyed. In your Starting Step, immediately before taking Company Morale Checks, you may elect to Destroy any or all Attacking platoons that are below half-strength. You may immediately bring the Destroyed platoons back again.

Treat the returning platoon as a totally new platoon. The old platoon still counts as being Destroyed for Company Morale Checks. If a platoon is Destroyed multiple times, it counts as multiple platoons being Destroyed.

New platoons do not add to the force's overall platoons for determining Victory Points.

TRENCH RESERVES

Trenches link the front line with the reserve area, allowing for reinforcements to get forward quickly and safely.

When a platoon arrives from Reserves, the owning player rolls a die to determine from which communication trench it will arrive. The mission map shows which trench the platoon will use for each roll. On a roll of 5 or 6, it will arrive anywhere along the owning player's table edge.

A platoon arriving from Reserves at a trench, arrives anywhere along the table edge within 6"/15cm of either side of the trench.

Sometimes there is not enough room in the trenches to bring on a whole platoon from reserve. In this case the remainder of the platoon will queue up in the communications trench, ready to come forward.

A platoon may leave teams off the table when it arrives from Reserves. These may enter the table from Reserves (automatically) in the same location as the rest of the platoon in subsequent turns.

FLANK ASSAULT

During a breakthrough, successful assaulting battalions would help adjacent ones clear their objectives to help widen the gap that had been created. These flank attacks helped the main assault push through difficult enemy positions.

In the Through Mud and Blood mission, the attacker must divide their force into two assaults: the Main Assault and the Flank Assault.

The Main Assault must include at least half of all of the attacker's platoons, which must include at least half of all of the attacker's Infantry platoons (those platoons containing only Infantry teams).

The Flank Assault must include at least one platoon, but no more than half of the total number of attacking platoons.

STRATEGIC RESERVES

Tanks

Tanks are rare and precious things and were not placed where the enemy's initial bombardments can hit them. When a force is placed on the defensive, most of its tanks are withdrawn and held well back, ready to counterattack the enemy.

The defender must hold all Armoured vehicles in Reserves (see page 268 of the rulebook).

Heavy Machine-guns

Heavy machine-guns are integrated into the front as well-concealed nests or hardened pillboxes. A reserve of heavy machine-guns could be brought up if needed.

The defending player may replace all of the HMG teams in any or all of their platoons with HMG bunkers. To do this the defender replaces:

- *one HMG team for an HMG Nest, or*
- *three HMG teams for an HMG Pillbox*

Doing this removes all other teams in the platoon from the game.

These Bunkers are Area Defences (see page 262 of the rulebook) and must be placed in the defenders Deployment Area at the start of the game before deployment.

Any HMG teams not replaced with HMG Nests or Pillboxes must be held in Reserves.

Guns and Artillery Batteries

Guns are deployed forward in well-protected positions to deal with the incoming enemy assault.

The defending player may place any or all Light, Medium, Heavy, or Immobile Gun teams in Gun Pits.

All Command Gun teams and any artillery batteries Deployed in Gun Pits or Trenches begin the game on the table.

All other platoons or batteries with Light, Medium, Heavy, or Immobile Gun teams must be held in Reserves.

All Remaining Platoons

The remainder of the defender's force is divided between the front line and the second line reserve. When the attack strikes the front, the reserves are committed to reinforce the defenders.

After all Tanks, Heavy Machine-guns, and Guns have been allocated to either be Deployed on the table or to be held in Reserves, at least half of all remaining platoons must be held in Reserves.

DECIDING WHO ATTACKS

New tactics and technology lead the way during Great War offensives. Meanwhile, the presence of an artillery battery this close to the front line means that your orders are to protect it at all costs.

A force that includes a German Artillery Battery (page 18), a British Field Battery, Royal Artillery (page 32), a French 75mm Artillery Battery (page 41), or an American Artillery Battery (page 50) Always Defends against all other companies, no matter what other platoons are in the same force.

All other forces that include Stoss Platoons (page 16) or any Tank teams Always Attack.

Otherwise, use the normal Deciding Who Attacks procedure found on page 257 of the rulebook.

GREAT WAR TABLE SIZE

Company-sized assaults were conducted on a narrow front to concentrate firepower against the defender's position.

Great War Missions are played on a 4'x4' (120cm x 120cm) table.

PLACING TRENCHES

Some missions use Trench Lines. The mission map will show you how to set up the trenches. When placing Trench Lines, you and your opponent may have to move or take away terrain to make room for them.

THE BIG PUSH
(DEFENSIVE BATTLE)

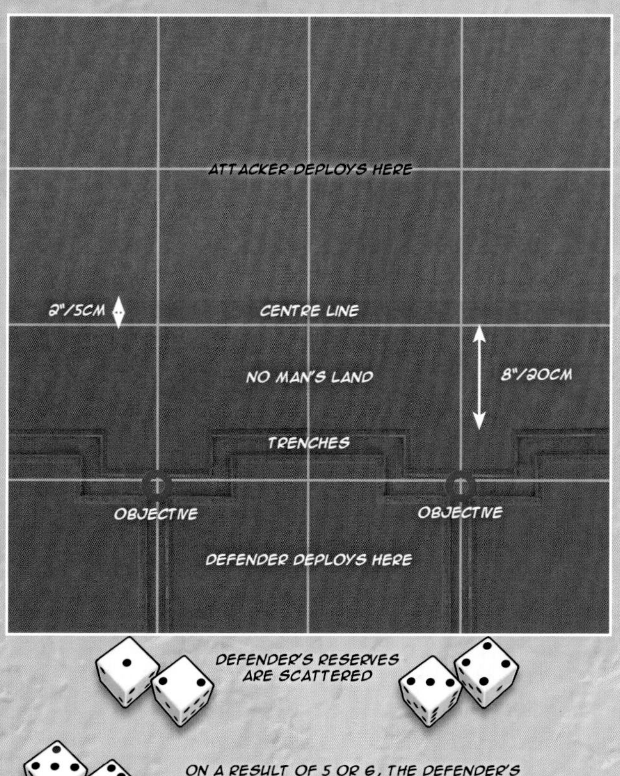

The Great War on the Western Front was dominated by set-piece attacks against well-prepared trench positions.

YOUR ORDERS

ATTACKER

You have been training for weeks in preparation for the big push. Fighting mock battles over an exact copy of the terrain you will fight over today. A massive barrage will lead your attack and you must punch through and blast open the enemy's defences.

DEFENDER

It has been quiet on the front for a few weeks, apart from the odd raid, and you suspect the enemy is up to something. You wait ready to repel any attack on your positions and to counterattack so that they don't gain any ground.

MISSION SPECIAL RULES

The Big Push uses the **Cratered Ground** (page 58), **Overwhelming Force** (page 58), **Preliminary Bombardment** (page 58), **Reserves** (page 268 of the rulebook), **Strategic Reserves** (page 59), and **Trench Reserves** (page 58) special rules.

PREPARING FOR BATTLE

1. The defending player chooses which table edge they will defend. Their Deployment Area is the part of this half of the table more than 8"/20cm from the centre line. The attacking player will attack from the other table half.
2. The defender now places the Trench Lines as shown and places up to six Barbed Wire Entanglements to span the table anywhere within No Man's Land.
3. The Objectives are the intersections between the front-line trench and the communications trenches running to the rear.
4. The defending player uses the Strategic Reserves rule to determine the platoons held in Reserves at the start of the game. These will arrive using the Trench Reserves special rule.
5. The defender Deploys their remaining platoons.
6. The attacking player's Deployment Area is their half of the table, excluding the area within 2"/5cm of the centre line. The attacker now Deploys all of their platoons.
7. Both players now Deploy any Warrior teams that are not part of a platoon and all Independent teams, starting with the defending player.

BEGINNING THE BATTLE

1. All defending platoons are Pinned Down from the Preliminary Bombardment (see page 58).
2. The entire table is Cratered Ground (see page 58).
3. The attacking player has the first turn.

ENDING THE BATTLE

The battle ends when either:

- the attacker starts any of their turns from turn six having Taken any of the Objectives, or
- the defender starts any of their turns from turn six with no attacking teams in the defender's trenches.

DECIDING WHO WON

The attacker wins if the game ended because they have Taken an Objective. They have broken the defence and forced the enemy to fall back to the second line.

Otherwise the defender wins. The attack has been beaten off. Now they must prepare their counter-stroke.

Calculate your Victory Points using the Victory Points Table on page 275 of the rulebook.

THROUGH THE MUD AND BLOOD
(MOBILE BATTLE)

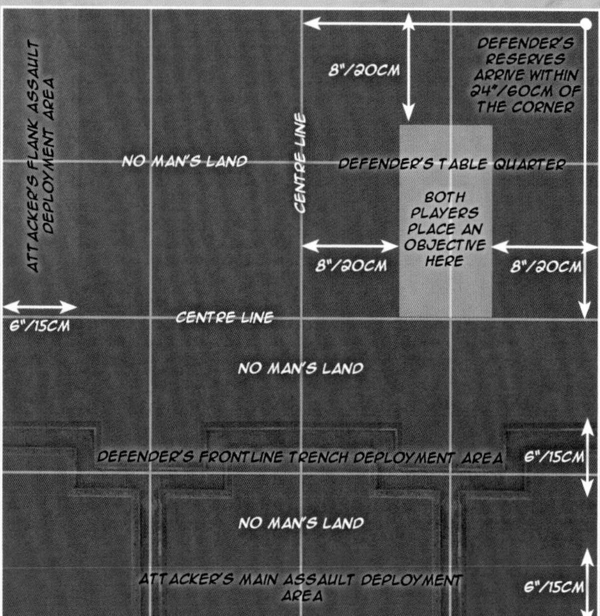

The forward trenches are taken, and the attacker pushes on. The fate of the operation hangs in the balance!

YOUR ORDERS

ATTACKER

Your forces have cleared the enemy's forward positions, and you are now poised to press into the second trench lines using the enemy's communication trenches for cover. To your left, your comrades have accomplished their assault and are turning in to meet yours. Join forces to secure the objective and push on to the green fields beyond.

DEFENDER

The enemy has broken through our forward trench line. The survivors and second-line troops are ready to slow them down long enough for your reserves to march forward and block the incoming attack.

MISSION SPECIAL RULES

Through the Mud and Blood uses the **Flank Assault** (page 58), **Reserves** (page 268 of the rulebook), and **Strategic Reserves** (page 59) special rules.

PREPARING FOR BATTLE

1. Mark the centre of the table so that the table quarters are obvious to both players.
2. The defending player chooses a table quarter as their Deployment Area for any Artillery Batteries in their force. Then the attacking player chooses an adjacent table quarter where their flank assault will be Deployed.
3. In the remaining table half, place Trench Lines as shown above. The defender now deploys all HMG nests or pillboxes in their force in the Frontline Trench Deployment Area, within 6"/15cm of the front of the trench line.
4. Starting with the defender, both players now place one Objective each in the defender's table quarter so that it is more than 8"/20cm of the table edges and more than 8"/20cm from the table centre line running parallel with the attacker's flank assault table edge.
5. The defender determines which platoons are Deployed on the table using the Strategic Reserves special rule. Platoons arriving from Reserves will do so within 24"/60cm of the corner of the defender's table quarter.
6. All of the defender's Artillery Batteries may be Deployed in the Defender's table quarter. All remaining platoons are Deployed in the Frontline Trench Deployment Area.
7. The area within 6"/15cm of the nearest table edge that runs parallel to the trenches is the Attacker's Main Assault Deployment Area. The area within 6"/15cm of the table edge opposite the defender's table quarter is the Attacker's Flank Assault Deployment Area.
8. The attacker now Deploys their force using the Flank Assault special rule (page 58).
9. Both players now Deploy any Warrior teams that are not part of a platoon and all Independent teams, starting with the defending player.

BEGINNING THE BATTLE

1. The defending player has the first turn.

ENDING THE BATTLE

The battle ends when either:

- the attacker has Taken any of the Objectives at the start of their turn, or
- the defender starts any of their turns from turn six with no attacking teams within 12"/30cm of an Objective.

DECIDING WHO WON

The attacker wins if the game ended because they have Taken an Objective. They have broken the front line and opened a way to the green fields beyond. Otherwise the defender wins. The attack has been repelled, allowing the defenders to plan a counterattack to gain back any lost ground.

Calculate your Victory Points using the Victory Points Table on page 275 of the rulebook.

THE GREEN FIELDS BEYOND
(FAIR FIGHT)

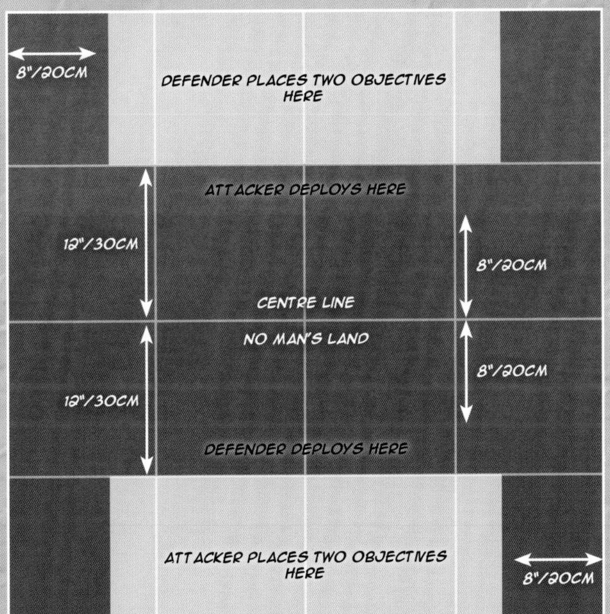

The objective of the 'Big Push' is to get through the enemy's trenches and into the open fields beyond.

YOUR ORDERS

ATTACKER

Your forces have broken through the enemy trenches. The enemy must be ruthlessly crushed before they can reoccupy their lost trenches! Seize your objectives before the enemy seizes one of their own.

DEFENDER

The enemy has broken through. Your company must launch an immediate counterattack to regain our lost trenches. Capture one of your Objectives before the enemy can take one of theirs.

MISSION SPECIAL RULES

The Green Fields Beyond uses the **Meeting Engagement** special rule (see page 264 of the rulebook).

PREPARING FOR BATTLE

1. Both players roll a die. The player with the higher score chooses a table edge to attack from. The other player defends from the opposite table edge.
2. Starting with the attacking player, both players place two Objectives on the opponent's side of the table. The Objectives must be at least 12"/30cm from the centre line of the table and may not be placed within 8"/20cm of the side table edges.
3. Each player's Deployment Area is their own half of the table, excluding the area within 8"/20cm of the table centre line. Both players, starting with the attacking player, alternate Deploying their platoons.
4. Both players, starting with the attacking player, now Deploy any Warrior teams that are not part of a platoon and all Independent teams.

BEGINNING THE BATTLE

1. Both players now roll a die. The player who finished Deploying their platoons first adds +1 to their roll. The player with the higher result has the first turn. In the event of a tie roll again.

ENDING THE BATTLE

The battle ends when:

- a player starts their turn having Taken either of the Objectives that they have placed in the enemy Deployment Area.

DECIDING WHO WON

The player that took their Objective has secured a key piece of terrain on the field, forcing the enemy onto the defensive and winning the day.

Calculate your Victory Points using the Victory Points Table on page 275 of the rulebook.

If neither side won use the There Are No Draws rule (see page 275 of the rulebook) to determine their Victory Points.

POCKET DEFENCE
(DEFENSIVE BATTLE)

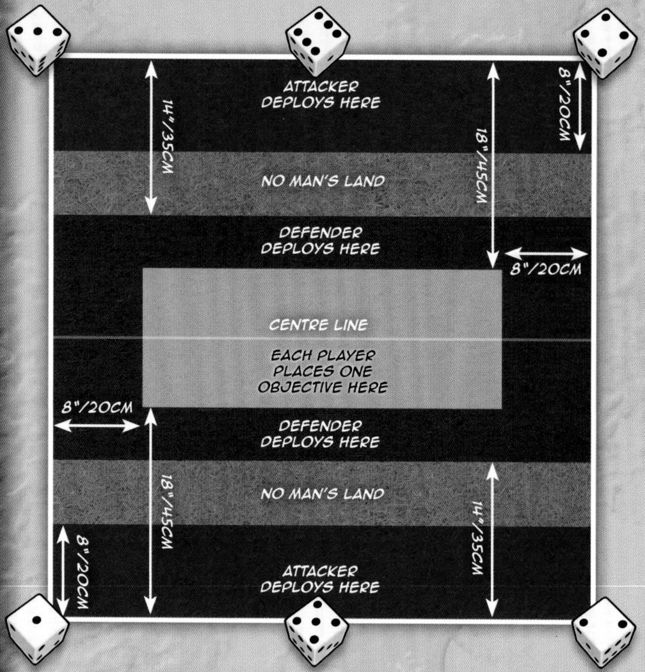

One army is cut off and surrounded behind enemy lines; but help is on its way. Can the defenders hunker down and hold off the attacker long enough for reinforcements to arrive or will the attackers crush this wayward enemy?

YOUR ORDERS

ATTACKER

Somehow the enemy has passed through our front lines, we believe they are cut off. Your mission is to attack them now before they can receive any further reinforcements.

DEFENDER

Being cut off from the main force you find yourself completely lost and surrounded. The bad news is the enemy knows you're here, the good news is help is on its way! You must hold your ground until the rest of our forces punch their way through to your position.

MISSION SPECIAL RULES

Pocket Defence uses the **Waylaid Reserves** (see below), **Scattered Reserves** (page 269 of the rulebook), **Preliminary Bombardment** (page 58), **Prepared Positions** (page 264 of the rulebook) special rules.

PREPARING FOR BATTLE

1. The Attack chooses a table edge to attack from. That and the opposite table edge define the Attackers deployment areas.
1. Starting with the defender, both players place an objective in the defenders deployment area so that it's more than 8"/20cm from any side table edge, and more than 18"/45cm from the Attacker's table edges.
2. The defender must place all their tanks in Waylaid Scattered Reserves. The Defender places his remaining platoons on the table more than 14"/35cm from the Attacker's table edges.
3. The attacking player now Deploys their entire force. They may Deploy their platoons in either part of their Deployment Area up to 8"/20 from either Attacker's table edge, but must Deploy at least one platoon in each half of their Deployment Area.
4. Starting with the defender, both players now Deploy any Warrior teams that are not part of a platoon and all Independent teams.

BEGINNING THE BATTLE

1. All defending platoons are Pinned Down from the Preliminary Bombardment.
2. The attacking player has first turn.

ENDING THE BATTLE

The battle ends when either:

- the Attacker starts any of their turns from turn six having Taken any Objectives, or
- the defender starts any of their turns from turn six with no attacking teams within 12"/30cm of any Objective.

DECIDING WHO WON

The attacker wins if the game ended because they started one of their turns holding an objective. The attacker has smashed the isolated enemy and seized their objectives.

Otherwise the defender wins. The isolated force has held out long enough for other units to link-up with them.

Calculate your Victory Points using the Victory Points Table on page 275 of the rulebook.

WAYLAID RESERVES

Your men have delved deep behind the enemy lines and are cut off. Disorientated, you know help is coming, but this far behind the enemy lines you are uncertain where they will show up.

Unlike normal Reserves you do not roll dice for Waylaid Reserves. Instead, at the beginning of turn three all models in Waylaid Reserves are placed on the table as if they had all arrived from Reserves.

Waylaid reserves are scattered. Only roll one dice for all the platoons arriving from Reserves to determine where they arrive.

Due to the smaller size of tables in Great War, Scattered Reserves arriving on a corner must enter the table within 12"/30cm of the corner (instead of 16"/40cm).

OVER THE TOP!
USING NORMAL FLAMES OF WAR MISSIONS IN THE GREAT WAR

The previous *Great War* missions (pages 61 to 63) cover three distinct, almost cinematic, missions. The story starts with the 'Big Push', the attacker closing in behind a rolling barrage and hitting the defender's forward trench line in force.

The next mission, Through Mud and Blood, carries on where the previous mission ends, with the attacker pushing into the second line of trenches. A supporting flank attack arrives to help push through while the Defender's reserves arrive to help stabilize the situation.

The last battle takes players into the 'Green fields beyond', where the attacker has pushed well beyond the trenches and the cratered ground. Indeed, many of the battles in 1918 were fought over such a landscape.

With these three missions, and the new Pocket Defence mission, players have a sample of the types of missions that the troops in the Great War would have been asked to accomplish. From there, we've modified the standard *Flames Of War* missions so that they fit on the smaller play area of Great War games and incorporate WWI-specific rules such as Strategic Reserves.

ADDING TRENCHES

Trenches are an iconic thing for Great War games. With the exception of the No Man's Land mission, the following do not include trenches, but you can add them to your table if you like. Keep in mind that doing so will have an impact on the game, so make sure that you run it by your opponent before getting started.

For some missions, how and where to place the trenches is pretty straight forward. For example, placing them in the defender's half of the table in a mission like No Retreat or Hold the Line, makes sense.

Other missions, like Breakthrough, can be difficult. In these sorts of missions, it might be best to either leave them off entirely or place them before choosing deployment areas, allowing the trenches to potentially run across both player's starting areas (representing a trench-clearing mission, perhaps.).

When placing trenches, you may have to move or take away terrain to make room for them.

GREAT WAR TABLE SIZE

Company-sized assaults were conducted on a narrow front to concentrate firepower against the defender's position. As such, Great War Missions are played on a 4'x4' (120cm x 120cm) table.

NO MAN'S LAND
(TRENCH WARFARE)

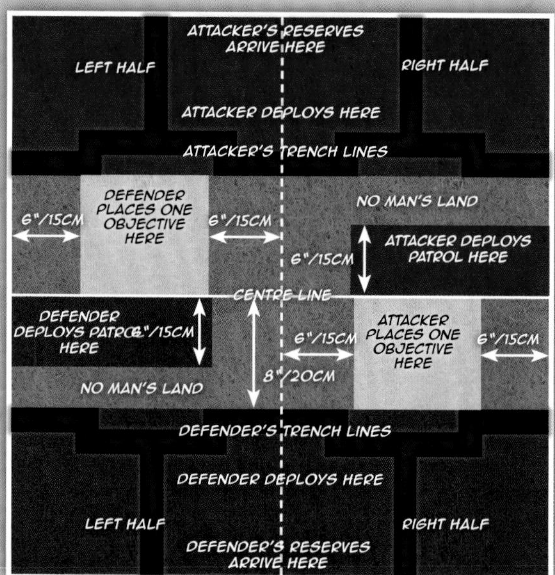

All is quiet in your fortified sector of the line. It seems like a good time to send out a patrol and see what the enemy is up to.

YOUR ORDERS

ATTACKER

Tonight's patrol ran into a strong enemy patrol. Reinforce them and secure the objective.

DEFENDER

Push the enemy out of No Man's Land and hold your objective.

Mission Special Rules

No Man's Land uses the **Darkness** (page 273 of the rulebook), **Delayed Reserves** (page 269 of the rulebook), **No Man's Land Patrol** (page 271 of the rulebook), **Over the Wire** (page 271 of the rulebook), and **Strategic Reserves** (page 59) special rules.

Preparing for Battle

1. Both players roll a die with the higher scoring player choosing a long table edge to attack from. The defender has the opposite table edge. The players' Deployment Areas are their halves of the table excluding the area within 8"/20cm of the centre line.
2. Both players now place Trench Lines as shown above on the mission map.
3. Again starting with the defender, both players place three Barbed Wire Entanglements in the opponent's table half using the Over The Wire mission special rule. However, place these at least 6"/15cm (rather than 8"/20cm) back from the table centre line.
4. Starting with the defender, both players use the Strategic Reserves rule to determine the platoons to be held off the table in Delayed Reserves. These will arrive anywhere along the table edge in their own Deployment Area.
5. Again starting with the defender, both players alternate deploying their remaining platoons in their Trenches or Gun Pits.
6. Starting with the attacker, both players nominate one platoon to be their Patrol using the No Man's Land Patrol special rule, and remove it from the table.
7. Divide the table into left and right halves across both Deployment Areas at right angles to the centre line.
8. Both players roll another die. The player with the higher score chooses the left or right half to place their Objective and Patrol. They place an Objective on the opposing side of the table at least 6"/15cm from the dividing line between the left and right halves, and at least 6"/15cm from the table edges.
9. The other player then places an Objective in the same manner in the opposite half.
10. The first player then places their Patrol on their side of the table in the same half as they placed the Objective, within 6"/15cm of the centre line and at least 6"/15cm from the dividing line between the left and right halves.
11. The other player then places their Patrol in the same manner in the opposite half.
12. Again starting with the defender, both players Deploy any Warrior teams that are not part of a platoon and all Independent teams in any Trench Lines in their Deployment Area.

Beginning the Battle

1. The entire battle is fought in Darkness.
2. Both players roll a die. The defender adds +1 to their roll. The player with the higher result has the first turn.

Ending the Battle

The battle ends when:

- a player starts their turn having Taken the Objective placed by the opposing player.

Deciding Who Won

The player that took an Objective wins the battle. They have established their dominance over No Man's Land.

Calculate your Victory Points using the Victory Points Table on page 275 of the rulebook.

No Man's Land is a Fair Fight, so if neither win the battle, use the There are No Draws rule on page 275 of the rulebook to determine each player's Victory Points.

DUST UP
(FAIR FIGHT)

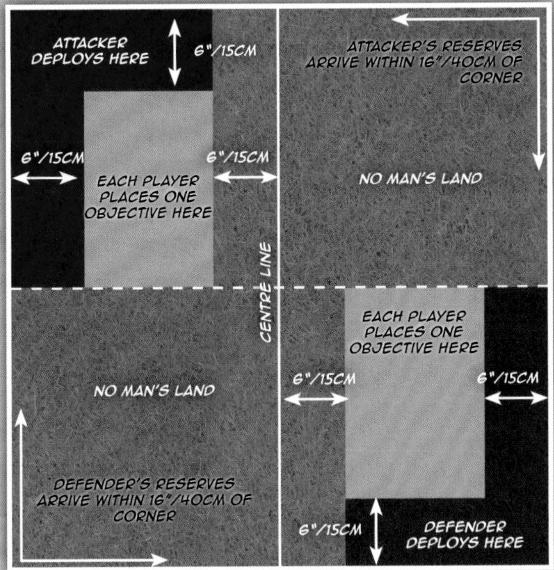

Two advancing forces clash, each determined to get through to their objectives. Soon a whirling battle develops as reserves arrive on the flanks and are thrown into the fray.

YOUR ORDERS

ATTACKER

You have encountered strong opposition and called for assistance, but so has the enemy. You must attack now while they are still weak and seize one of your objectives before the enemy captures one of theirs.

DEFENDER

Parry your opponents thrust and manoeuvre your forces to take and hold a key position behind their lines. Be ready to attack when the time is right. Strike hard and fast to take an objective before the enemy does so.

MISSION SPECIAL RULES

Dust Up uses the **Delayed Reserves** (page 269 of the rulebook) and **Meeting Engagement** (page 264 of the rulebook), and **Strategic Reserves** (page 59) special rules.

PREPARING FOR BATTLE

1. Mark the centre of the table so that the table quarters are obvious to both players.
2. Both players roll a die. The player with the higher score chooses a table quarter to attack from, leaving the other table quarter in their own end empty.
3. The other player deploys in the opposite table quarter, likewise leaving the other table quarter in their own end empty. Each player's Deployment Area is their assigned quarter, excluding the area within 6"/15cm of the centre line.
4. Starting with the attacker each player places an objective in their own Deployment Area at least 6"/15cm from all table edges.
5. Next starting with the attacker each player places an objective in the enemy Deployment Area at least 6"/15cm from all table edges.
6. Starting with the attacker, both players use the Strategic Reserves rule to determine the platoons held off the table in Delayed Reserves.
7. Each player's Reserves arrive up to 16"/40cm from the corner in the empty table quarter at the enemy's end of the table.
8. Both players, starting with the attacker, alternate Deploying platoons.
9. Again starting with the attacker, both players now Deploy any Warrior teams that are not part of a platoon and all Independent teams.

BEGINNING THE BATTLE

Both players now roll a die. The player who finished Deploying their platoons first adds +1 to their roll. The player with the higher result has the first turn. In the event of a tie roll again.

ENDING THE BATTLE

The battle ends when:

- a player starts their turn having Taken either of the Objectives that were placed in the enemy Deployment Area.

DECIDING WHO WON

The player that took an Objective in the opponent's Deployment Area wins the battle. They have secured key terrain, opening the way for the decisive blow.

Calculate your Victory Points using the Victory Points Table on page 275 of the rulebook.

If neither side won use the There are No Draws special rule (page 275 of the rulebook) to determine their Victory Points.

German Painting Guide

German Paint List

Uniform and Putees

GRENADIER GREEN (349)

Helmet, Gasmask Tin, Guns / Mortars

HEER GREEN (340)

Boots, Belt

BOOT BROWN (323)

Web Equipment, Pistol holsters, Officer's Boots

BLACK (300)

Canteens

WOOL BROWN (328)

Bread Bag, Grenade Sacks

WORN CANVAS (306)

Rifles, Entrenching Tool Handles

BATTLEFIELD BROWN (341)

The painting guides in this book are specifically suited to the unique camouflage and colour schemes used by the armies of the Great War. More general techniques and step-by-step guides can be found in *Colour Of War*.

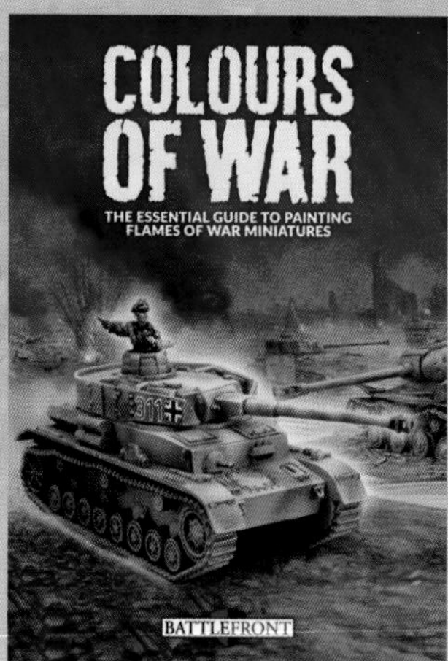

Colours Of War is a detailed and comprehensive book with practical information and techniques to help you paint all of your *Flames Of War* miniatures. The detailed guides are designed to work with seamlessly with the *Colours Of War* range of acylic paints and washes. Find the *Colours Of War* painting guide book and paints in stores now.

German Infantry

Colour Palette

GRENADIER GREEN (349)

HEER GREEN (340)

MANSTEIN SHADE (492)

WORN CANVAS (306)

If you have painted World War II German infantry, their Great War predecessors will not pose much of a challenge. Although the design of most items of the uniform and equipment are somewhat different, the colours are very similar.

GRENADIER GREEN — *Large Brush*

BASECOAT *the uniform with Grenadier Green.*

HEER GREEN — *Medium Brush*

BASECOAT *the helmet, mess tin and grenade heads with Heer Green.*

MANSTEIN SHADE — *Large Brush*

WASH *the figure liberally with Manstein Shade to create shading.*

GRENADIER GREEN — *Medium Brush*

PAINT *the uniform Grenadier Green, leaving darker shading in the recesses.*

75% HEER GREEN / 25% GRENADIER GREEN — *Small Brush*

HIGHLIGHT *the helmet, mess tin and grenade heads with a mix of Heer Green and Grenadier Green.*

75% GRENADIER GREEN / 25% WORN CANVAS — *Small Brush*

HIGHLIGHT *the edges and raised areas of the uniform with a mix of Grenadier Green and Worn Canvas.*

Painting Tank Camouflage

German Tank Camouflage

Colour Palette

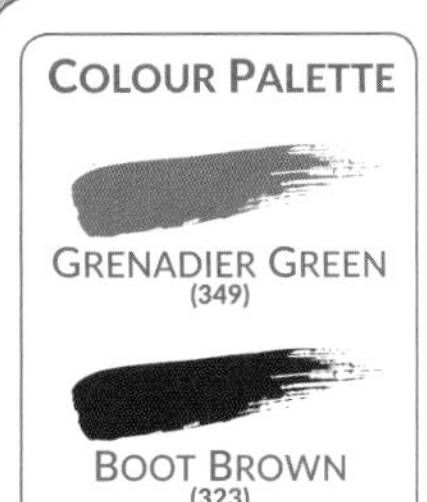

Grenadier Green (349)

Boot Brown (323)

Sicily Yellow (362)

Photographs show a number of different paint schemes on German A7V tanks. But this three-colour soft-edged pattern seems to have been the most common. Using an airbrush is an ideal way to paint soft-edged patterns, but they can also be achieved very effectively by hand, using a stippling technique.

Grenadier Green – *Large Brush*

Basecoat *the tank using Grenadier Green. You may want to add additional shading using a wash of Manstein Shade.*

Boot Brown – *Medium Brush*

Paint *uneven cloud shapes in Boot Brown. Make the shapes a little smaller at first, to leave room to enlarge them in the next step.*

Boot Brown – *Small Drybrush*

Stipple *soft edges around the patches to create a sprayed-on look. Page 15 of Colours Of War has more information about the stippling technique.*

Sicily Yellow – *Small Drybrush*

Repeat *the last two steps to add similar sized cloudy patches of Sicily Yellow.*

French Tank Camouflage

Colour Palette

Luftwaffe Blue (401)

Whitewash (307)

Dry Dust (364)

Motherland Earth (383)

Army Green (342)

Black (300)

This camouflage pattern might look complex, but it is actually not difficult if you are patient and methodical.

50% Luftwaffe Blue, 50% Whitewash – *Large Brush*

Basecoat *the vehicle with a mix of Luftwaffe Blue and Whitewash.*

Dry Dust – *Medium Brush*

Paint *wavy cloud shapes in Dry Dust, aiming to cover around 20% of the vehicle's surface.*

Motherland Earth – *Medium Brush*

Add *more wavy cloud shapes with Motherland Earth.*

Army Green – *Medium Brush*

Repeat *the previous two steps, this time using Army Green.*

Luftwaffe Blue – *Medium Brush*

Add *slightly smaller cloud shapes with pure Luftwaffe Blue.*

Black – *Small Brush*

Outline *the borders between each colour with a thin line of Black.*

French Painting Guide

French Metropolitan Infantry

Colour Palette

Luftwaffe Blue (401)

Infantry Blue (400)

Manstein Shade (492)

Military Khaki (327)

A 'tricolour' cloth was created from a patriotic mix of red, white and blue threads, resulting in a dull khaki colour. But the only source of the necessary red dye was Germany. The blue and white threads alone created the pale blue colour which came to be known as 'horizon blue'.

Basecoat *the uniform with a mix of Luftwaffe Blue and Infantry Blue.*

Basecoat *the helmet with Luftwaffe Blue.*

Wash *the figure liberally with Manstein Shade to add shading and definition.*

Paint *the uniform with the blue basecoat mix, tidying up the wash while leaving darker recesses.*

Tidy Up *the shading on the helmet with Luftwaffe Blue.*

Highlight *the uniform by adding a small amout of Military Khaki to the blue basecoat mix.*

French Infantry

Metropolitan Helmets
Luftwaffe Blue (401)

Metropolitan Helmets
Luftwaffe Blue (401)
Infantry Blue (400)

Webbing & Pouches
Military Khaki (327)

Or
Sicily Yellow (362)

Boots
Black (300)

Officer's Boots
Boot Brown (323)

Metropolitan Infantry

Colonial Infantry

Colonial Helmets
Battledress Brown (325)

Colonial Uniform
Battledress Brown (325)

Canteen & Rifle Wood
Battlefield Brown (341)

Rifles, SMGs, & MGs
Dark Gunmetal (480)

British & American Painting Guide

British and American Infantry

While the design was different, the colours of the British and American uniforms and equipment were similar enough that most of the same paints and techniques can be used for both.

Basecoat *the uniform Battlefield Brown, in two thin coats if necessary to achieve an even coverage.*

Basecoat *the helmet with Sherman Drab.*

Wash *the figure with Monty Shade to add shading and give the uniform the correct greenish tone.*

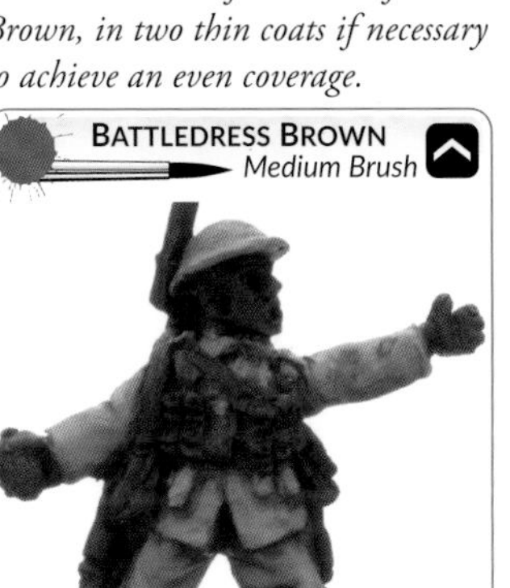

Paint *the uniform with Battledress Brown, leaving dark shadows in the recessed areas.*

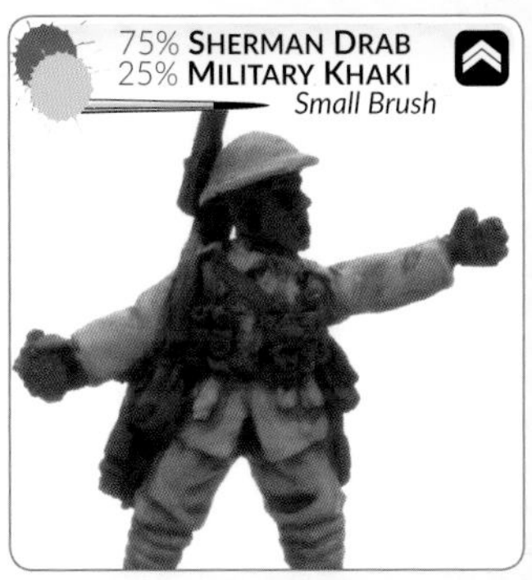

Highlight *the helmet with a mix of Sherman Drab and Military Khaki.*

Highlight *the edges and raised areas of the uniform for a brighter, higher contrast look.*

British & American Paint List

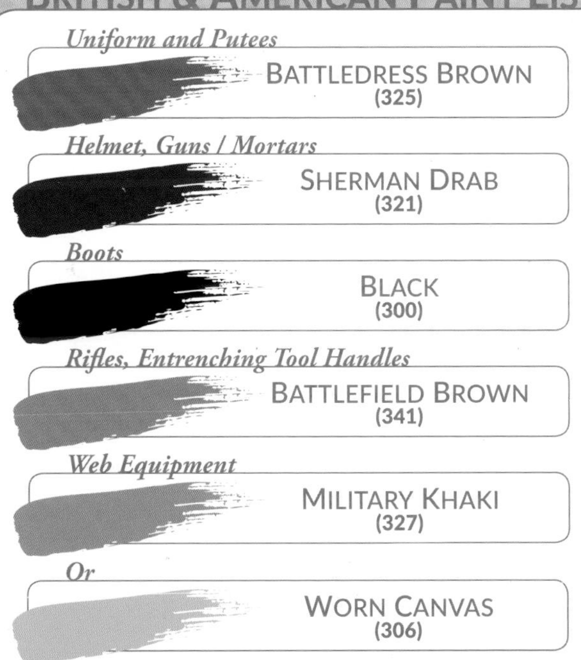

THE GREAT WAR BATTLEFIELD

Battlefields of the Great War varied from the classic mud of Flanders to the pristine green fields beyond the touch of war. Here are a few guidelines for constructing a unique Great War battlefield.

Trenches

Perhaps the most iconic symbol of World War I is the trench. Starting from simple slit trenches and developing into elaborate trench networks such as the Hindenburg Line, the science of entrenchment was king of the battlefield.

Trenches follow all of the usual Entrenchments rules found in the rulebook (see page 4 and page 215 of the rulebook).

Teams assaulting into Trenches use the Push into Enemy Positions rule (page 160 of the rulebook).

Barbed Wire

Like trenches, endless lines of barbed wire are an essential part of the Great War battlefield.

Barbed Wire Entanglements use all of the usual Barbed Wire Entanglements rules found in the rulebook (see page 227).

Muddy Ground

The 1918 Spring Offensives encountered some wet weather, producing patches or whole battlefields of mud (though not on the same scale as 1916 and 1917).

You can either designate patches of your battlefield as Muddy or choose to call the whole battlefield Muddy.

Muddy terrain is Slow Going to all teams.

Shattered Woods

Many battlefields had some woods that were utterly destroyed by shelling and fighting or cleared to provide a field of fire for machine-guns. These woods still provide some cover.

Shattered Woods are Slow Going for all teams trying to pass through. A Shattered Wood is not a normal wood. Instead, Infantry and Man-packed gun teams inside a Shattered Wood are Concealed.

Ruined Villages

Many battlefields were fought over strategically important villages. Some of those villages have been shelled into oblivion, creating an ideal battlefield for infantry.

A Ruined Village uses the normal rules for ruins and buildings found in the rulebook.